100 HARLEYS

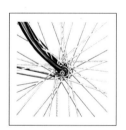

100 HARLEYS

TOD RAFFERTY'S 100 HOTTEST HARLEYS

TOD RAFFERTY

THUNDER BAY
P·R·E·S·S

CREDITS

PHOTOGRAPHER Neil Sutherland   EDITOR Philip de Ste. Croix   DIRECTOR OF EDITORIAL Will Steeds   DESIGN Louise Clements
DESIGN MANAGER Justina Leitão   PRODUCTION Neil Randles, Karen Staff

Published in the United States by
Thunder Bay Press
An imprint of the Advantage Publishers Group
5880 Oberlin Drive, San Diego, CA 92121-4794
www.advantagebooksonline.com

All notations of errors or omissions should be addressed to
Thunder Bay Press, editorial department, at the above address.
All other correspondence (author inquiries, permissions)
concerning the content of this book should be addressed to
Salamander Books Limited, 8 Blenheim Court, Brewery Road,
London N7 9NY, England.

Library of Congress Cataloging-in-Publication Data available
upon request.
ISBN 1-57145-564-7

Produced by Toppan
Printed in China

1 2 3 4 5 01 02 03 04

Tod Rafferty

Tod Rafferty is a veteran motorcycle junkie and former editor of *Cycle News*, *Big Bike* magazine, and contributing editor for *Cycle Guide* magazine. He was also automotive editor of the *Telegram-Tribune* newspaper in San Luis Obispo, California. The author's previous works include *Harley-Davidson: The Ultimate Machine* (Running Press, 1994), *The Complete Harley-Davidson* (Motorbooks International, 1997), *Harley Memorabilia* (Chartwell Books, 1997), and *The Indian* (CLB, 1998).

CONTENTS

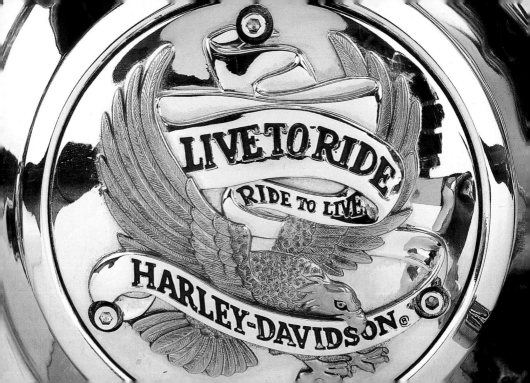

INTRODUCTION

The Harley-Davidson Motor Company celebrates its centennial in 2003. In anticipation of this milestone we present 100 Harleys, in tribute to a century of motorcycle production from Milwaukee, Wisconsin. The machines and mementos pictured here represent a condensed history of American motorcycling, and a handy guidebook for fans of the longest-running manufacturer in the business.

1902 WILLIAM S. Harley and Arthur Davidson complete the first actual Harley-Davidson engine, its 3-inch (76mm) bore and 3½-inch (89mm) stroke producing three horse-power. Arthur's brother, Walter Davidson, has returned from Kansas for the wedding of the third brother, William. When Walter, a machinist, and William Davidson, a toolmaker, join the team, the Harley-Davidson Motor Company is on the road.

1903 THE FIRST Harley-Davidson production motorcycle is made, followed by two more. Each single-cylinder, belt-drive machine has been sold in advance.

1904 PRODUCTION AGAIN totals three machines, now nicknamed the Silent Gray Fellow. The conservative color and and quiet muffler indicate Milwaukee's interest in social acceptance for the new machines.

1905 THE FIRST outside employee is hired, production rises to seven. Engines are sold separately, and carburetors, boat motors and propellers are added to the catalog.

1906 A DAVIDSON uncle, James McLay, finances construction of a new plant on the site that becomes Harley-Davidson's permanent location. The Juneau Avenue factory adds five more employees and production increases to 50 motorcycles. William Harley takes leave of absence to study engineering at the University of Wisconsin.

1907 HARLEY-DAVIDSON becomes a corporation, with shares divided among 17 employees. Total production rises to 150 machines, among them the first sold for use by the police.

1908   A PROTOTYPE of the first 1000cc V-twin wins a hillclimb in Algonquin,
Illinois. More factory space is added and overall production climbs to 410.
Walter Davidson wins the 365-mile Federation
of American Motorcyclists endurance run in
New York with a perfect score.

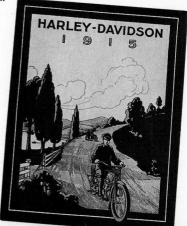

1909   THE 7-HORSEPOWER, 45-degree V-twin is
produced to compete with the popular Indian.
Valve train design proves inadequate, and the
twin is withdrawn for more development.

1911   THE TWIN is reintroduced with
mechanical valves and a new frame.
Belt drive remains standard.

1912 THE V-TWIN gets chain drive and a rear wheel clutch. The Full-Floteing Seat, designed by Bill Harley, features center-post suspension. Seven people die at a New Jersey motordrome racing accident.

1913 A NEW 5-horsepower, 35 cubic inch (565cc) single is offered with belt or chain drive. Also new is a two-speed rear hub. William Ottaway, formerly of Thor Motorcycles, is hired as manager of the new Harley-Davidson racing team.

1914 THE KICKSTARTER and internal expanding rear brake are new features. Volume sales are made to the U.S. Army and postal service.

1915 IMPROVEMENTS INCLUDE a three-speed transmission and engine clutch. Otto Walker and Red Parkhurst, of the Harley Wrecking Crew, finish 1-2 in the 300-mile race at Venice, California. The delivery sidevan debuts.

1916 MILWAUKEE OFFERS 11-horsepower V-twins for racing at $250. Military sidecars are equipped with machine gun mounts for use on the Mexican border and the war in Europe.

1917 THE U.S. enters the war and H-D converts to military production. The factory service school is established to train mechanics for the war effort.

1918 WORLD WAR I ends in November. Dispatch rider Roy Holtz, of Chippewa Falls, Wisconsin, is the first American to enter Germany. He is riding a Harley-Davidson with a sidecar.

1919 H-D INTRODUCES the 36 cubic inch (584cc) Model W, a horizontally opposed sport twin. Unlike any Harley before or since, the model was unsuccessful and was discontinued after four years. Overall production in Milwaukee rises to more than 22,000 motorcycles and 16,000 sidecars.

1920 TEAM RIDER Red Parkhurst sets new speed records at Daytona Beach, Florida. Mass production of cars depresses motorcycle sales. Harley-Davidson begins new ad campaign to counteract negative public image of motorcycles. Harley dealerships exist in 67 countries around the world.

1921 H-D PRODUCTION drops to 10,000 machines. Sidecars get increased emphasis in company advertising.

Next Door to the Great Outdoors

1922 THE 74 CUBIC inch (1200cc) side-valve F model V-twin appears, rated at 18 horsepower. Military olive green replaced by brighter green with gold striping. Harley ads focus on growing number of women riders.

1923 FACTORY RACING team discontinued. The company catalog of clothing and accessories gets new emphasis, as does an aggressive financing plan.

1925 THE TEARDROP fuel tank is part of the "Stream-Line" models, offered at reduced prices. A new 21 cubic inch (350cc) side-valve single is added to the line.

1929 THE SECOND generation of Davidsons, and a Harley, join the firm. The 45 cubic inch (750cc) side-valve V-twin DL model debuts at $290. The new twin-cam 74 cubic inch(1200cc) JDH twin is $370. The Great Depression descends.

1930 REMOVABLE RICARDO cylinder heads for twins and singles, plus larger brakes and dual beam headlights. Bill Davidson, son of company Vice President, wins the 420-mile Jack Pine Tour in Michigan.

1931   THE THREE-WHEELED Servi-Car appears and commercial markets grow in importance.

1933   DEPRESSION DEEPENS; Milwaukee cuts back to a two-day work week.

1935   HARLEY RACER Joe Petrali wins every national dirt-track race of the year. Milwaukee displays new 61 cubic inch (1000cc) ohv Model E Knucklehead and 80 cubic inch (1340cc) side-valve VLH for 1936.

1937   JOE PETRALI rides the Knucklehead to a new speed record of 136mph (219kph) at Daytona. Founder William A. Davidson dies at age 66.

1940   THE 45 (750), 74 (1200) and 80 cubic inch (1340cc) engines get aluminum heads. More military versions of 750 shipped to England and Russia. The 74 cubic inch (1200cc) ohv FL model readied for release in 1941.

1941   CIVILIAN PRODUCTION ceases at year's end;
U.S. enters World War II. Harley-Davidson builds
nearly 90,000 WLA models for the military.
BMW-style shaft-drive horizontally opposed
twin XA model developed for desert
warfare; only 1,000 made.

1942   COMPANY PRESIDENT
Walter Davidson
dies, followed the next
year by William
Harley. Only
Arthur Davidson
remains of the
founding four.

1947   FULL CIVILIAN production resumes with updated 1941 models.
Accessories and clothing catalog grows larger; first appearance of zippered
black leather jacket. Motorcycle gangs get increasing publicity.

1948   THE 125 MODEL S debuts, a 125cc two-stroke based on DKW
design. The big twins get hydraulic lifters, and the Knucklehead is discontinued
in favor of the new 74 cubic inch (1200cc) Panhead. Production numbers
rise significantly.

1949   THE HYDRA-GLIDE arrives, an FL with telescopic forks and deeply
valanced fenders.

1950   ARTHUR DAVIDSON, 69, and his wife die in an automobile accident.

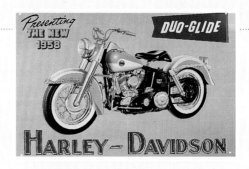

1952 THE K MODEL, a 45 cubic inch (750cc) side-valve V-twin, replaces the venerable WL. Unit construction gears, hand clutch and footshift make the racing KR model an instant success.

1953 MILWAUKEE CELEBRATES 50th anniversary. The 125cc Model S grows to 165cc.

1954 THE K MODEL becomes the KH at 54 cubic inches (883cc), forerunner to the Sportster

1956 LEROY WINTERS wins the Jack Pine on a 165. Elvis Presley buys a red and white KH model.

1957   KH BECOMES the XL Sportster with overhead valves.

1958   THE FL EVOLVES as the Duo-Glide with swingarm
suspension and hydraulic rear brake.
The Sportster gets more horsepower.

1959   CARROLL RESWEBER wins second of four straight
racing titles for Harley-Davidson. Honda 50cc
mini-bikes appear in U.S.

1960   MILWAUKEE BUYS half interest in
Aermacchi of Italy and imports the
Sprint, a 250cc four-stroke single.
Harley KR riders sweep top 14 places
in the Daytona 200.

1963 WILLIAM G. DAVIDSON, eldest son of William H., joins the company as director of styling.

1965 THE DUO-GLIDE gets electric start and becomes Electra-Glide.

1966 NEW ENGINE, known as the Shovelhead, fitted in the Electra-Glide. New cams and carburetor give the Sportster more grunt, and electric start for '67.

1968 CAL RAYBORN rides KR to Daytona victory, first to average more than 100mph (161kph).

1969 HARLEY-DAVIDSON sold to conglomerate American Machine and Foundry (AMF). Rayborn repeats win at Daytona.

1970 RAYBORN SETS world record of 265mph (426kph) at Bonneville in Sportster-powered streamliner. KR replaced by XR 750 developed by Dick O'Brien.

1971 AMF LOGO added to gas tanks. FX 1200 Super Glide debuts, a Willie G. design. Evel Knievel jumps to fame.

1972 SPORTSTER GROWS to 61 cubic inches (1000cc). Mark Brelsford regains national title on XR 750. Electra-Glide gets front disc brake.

1973 ASSEMBLY OPERATIONS moved from Milwaukee to AMF plant in York, Pennsylvania. William H. Davidson retires.

1975   THE SPRINT is dropped. Walter Villa wins second of three consecutive roadracing titles on Aermacchi RR 250.

1976   RELATIONS DETERIORATE between Harley-Davidson management, labor and AMF directors. Quality control suffers. H-D releases Liberty editions to mark U.S.A. bicentennial.

1977   WILLIE G. presents the Sportster-based XLCR Cafe Racer and FXS Low Rider version of Super Glide. Jay Springsteen wins first of three Grand National titles on XR 750.

1978   ELECTRA-GLIDE grows to 80 cubic inches (1340cc). H-D celebrates 75th birthday.

1979   TWO-STROKE production discontinued. Willie G. offers limited edition Electra-Glide Classic with sidecar. AMF looks to sell Harley-Davidson.

1980   THE FLT Tour Glide and Wide Glide factory custom premier, and the FXB Sturgis with belt drive.

1981   H-D MANAGERS, led by AMF executive Vaughn Beals, purchase Harley from AMF in leveraged buy-out.

1982   PRESIDENT RONALD Reagan grants Harley-Davidson relief from imported competition, puts 45 percent tariff on Japanese heavyweights. FXR Super Glide II gets rubber-mount engine, five-speed transmission.

1983   HARLEY OWNERS Group (H.O.G.) inaugurated. H-D legal department goes after trademark infringers. FXRT sport tourer gets air fork and computer controlled ignition.

1984   Introduction of 80 cubic inch
(1340cc) Evolution engine, and
XR-1000 Sportster. The FX Softail
debuts. Harley-Davidson regains
California Highway Patrol contract.

1986   Harley-Davidson contributes
$250,000 for Statue of Liberty
renovation. The XLH-883 Sportster
883cc Evolution debuts, at $3,995. The
FL Heritage Softail blends new technology
with 1950s look. Company goes public
with 2 million shares of common stock.
Harley-Davidson acquires Holiday Rambler,
a motorhome manufacturer.

1987 ELECTRA-GLIDE Sport, Heritage Softail Classic and Low Rider Custom are unveiled, and 30th Anniversary 1100cc Sportster. President Reagan visits York plant. Harley-Davidson listed on the New York Stock Exchange.

1988 SPORTSTER GROWS to 1200cc. Springer Softail celebrates 85th anniversary. Milwaukee festivities raise $600,000 for Muscular Dystrophy Association.

1990 THE FLSTF Fat Boy appears, another Willie G. retro-style. New Dyna Glide Sturgis shown at 50th Black Hills Classic in Sturgis, South Dakota. Attendance reaches 250,000-plus.

1991 SPORTSTERS GET five-speeds and belt drive. Scott Parker wins fourth Grand National title in a row, equalling Caroll Resweber's feat. HOG chapters reach 650 worldwide.

1992 The FX DAYTONA and Custom models get new Dyna Glide frame, Sportster Hugger features lower ride height. Chris Carr wins Grand National Championship.

1993 NEW DYNA Wide Glide has factory fitted Ape Hanger handlebars. Heritage Softail Nostalgia has cowhide inserts on seat and bags. Limited edition of Sportster, Low Rider, Wide-, Electra-, and Tour Glide commemorate Harley-Davidson 90th anniversary. Milwaukee hosts huge birthday party.

1994 VR 1000 roadracer debuts. New models include Low Rider Convertible, Heritage Softail Classic and Road King.

1995   RETRO BECOMES more active with the introduction of the FXSTSB, the
Softail Bad Boy. The springer fork carries history forward.

1996   THE SPORTSTER lineup grows to five with the addition of the XL 1200S Sport and
XL 1200C Custom. All get improved transmissions.

1998   HARLEY-DAVIDSON'S 95th birthday produces eight Anniversary editions and a big
party in Milwaukee. The discontinued Tour Glide is reincarnated as the FLTRI
Road Glide, with a new frame-mount fairing. The Sportster 1200S is fitted with a
new ignition system, and the Road King Classic is added to the roster.

1999   THE BIG news for 1999 is the Twin Cam 88, Milwaukee's first new engine since the
Evolution. The larger bore and shorter stroke signals quicker power delivery, and
new combustion chambers and improved lubrication indicate even more ponies can
be made. H-D announces production target for 1999 of 160,000 motorcycles.

CHAPTER 1

EARLY YEARS

The bicycle heritage is
apparent in the frame and
pedals of the early Harley-
Davidson singles.

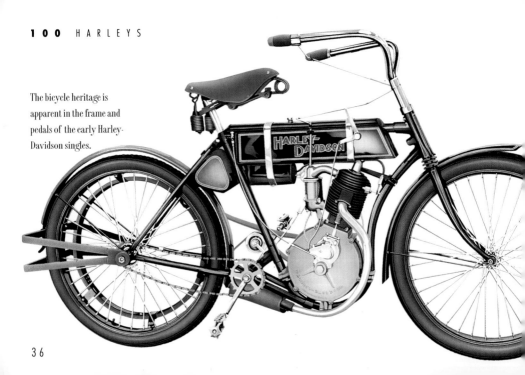

Single **1903**

The first prototype Harley-Davidson was actually begun in 1901. Since both William S. Harley, 21, and Arthur Davidson, 20, worked full-time for the same company, the after-hours project would consume most of the next two years of their lives. Soon they were captivated by the challenge of this newfangled device called a motorcycle. And their abilities, plus the support of friends and family, were to cast their futures in iron and steel. In 1903 they formally became The Harley-Davidson Motor Company.

The premier machine was basically a bicycle frame fitted with a single-cylinder four-stroke engine, with direct belt drive to the rear wheel. Though its performance was weak, the engine did produce enough power, and added weight, to point up the shortcomings of the bicycle chassis. So William and Arthur returned to the drawing table in search of both added power and durability. Bill Harley designed a stronger loop frame to accommodate the new 24.74 cubic inch (405cc) engine, and the first genuine Harley-Davidson motorcycle was born.

SINGLE 1903

Engine IOE single
Displacement 24.74ci (405cc)
Transmission Direct drive
Horsepower Approx. 3
Wheelbase 51in (1295mm)
Weight 178lb (81kg)
Top speed Approx. 35mph (56kph)
Price $200

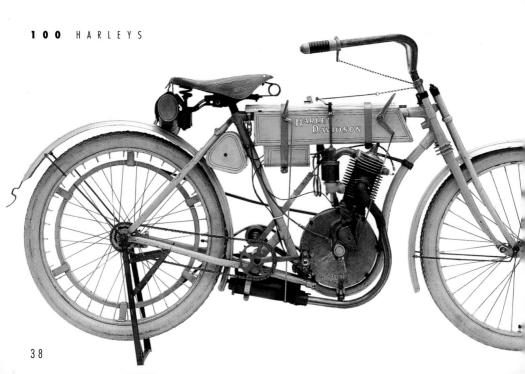

Single **1906-07**

By 1906 The Motor Company was well on its way to prosperity, which everyone agreed was just around the corner. Production increased to 50 motorcycles, and the first color option appeared on the order forms. Renault gray was the new hue, complemented by carmine red lettering on the tank and red pin-striping. With new paint came a new nickname, and advertising slogan, for the Harley-Davidson motor-cycle: The Silent Gray Fellow.

Motorcycling was already straining for respectability, and Milwaukee meant to lead the way as a responsible manufacturer. The business had grown quickly, and Harley-Davidson was busy on all fronts, with research on new ideas and designs, a national advertising campaign and the first real factory on Chestnut Street, which would later become Juneau Avenue.

The motorcycle also showed signs that Harley-Davidson was in earnest about getting the job done. Having established something of a reputation for stout construction and durability, attention

SINGLE 1906-7

Engine IOE single
Displacement 26.8ci (440cc)
Transmission Direct drive
Horsepower Approx. 4
Wheelbase 51in (1295mm)
Weight 185lb (84kg)
Top speed Approx. 40mph (64kph)
Price $210

RIGHT: An original drawing, dated November 18, 1907, by William Harley for a Harley-Davidson spring fork. FAR RIGHT: A 1.25-inch (3.175cm) leather belt took engine power to the rear wheel. The leather-lined engine pulley was offered in three diameters.

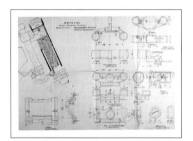

turned to making the motorcycle more user-friendly. The most prominent change came with the adoption of front suspension, in the form of the Sager-Cushion fork. The dual-spring, leading link assembly helped smooth the rutted and rocky roads and absorbed a portion of the impact heretofore delivered to the unfortunate rider.

With improved handling came a corresponding boost in power. An eighth-inch (0.32cm) increase in the cylinder bore brought displacement to 26.8 cubic inches (440cc), and the invigorating top speed of 45mph (72kph). In 1907 production jumped to 154 motorcycles, and the Harley-Davidson Motor Company was incorporated, with sales of $35,000 in stock limited to the 18 employees.

Arthur and Walter Davidson quit their

regular jobs to devote their full efforts to the family business. Their older brother William soon followed suit, and was appointed vice president and works manager. Bill Harley was chief engineer and treasurer, Arthur Davidson became sales manager and secretary, and Walter Davidson was the company's first president.

Walter and William Davidson were the most mechanically minded of the founding four, and paid close attention to the newest techniques in manufacturing and assembly. Together they went to Chicago to learn oxy-acetylene welding and trained their employees in the latest methods. Arthur was busy setting up a national network of Harley-Davidson dealers, while Bill Harley took time from his studies to start on the design of the company's first V-twin engine.

But it was Walter Davidson, the middle brother, who seemed to suddenly develop a talent that would gain a national reputation for the young company. The first of the Scots' immigrant family to be born in the U.S.A., Walter turned out to be one hell of a motorcycle rider.

LEFT: The leather saddle featured coil suspension. BELOW: A spring-loaded belt tensioner served as an early form of a clutch.

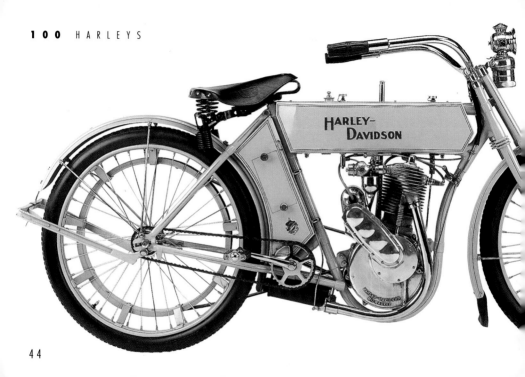

Model 5A **1909**

The Model 5A featured a new style of fuel tank which fitted flush with the frame.

After five years in the motorcycle business, Harley-Davidson was ready to take its place as an industry leader. The combined strategies of cautiously deliberate development, a network of trustworthy dealers and increased advertising were beginning to pay dividends.

The single, now designated the model 5, was the basic version; with battery and 28-inch (71cm) wheels, it was still priced at $210. The 5A pictured here, equipped with a Bosch magneto, was a hefty $40 more and only 54 were built. The factory also offered B and C models

MODEL 5A 1909

Engine IOE single
Displacement 30.16ci (494cc)
Transmission Direct drive
Horsepower 4.3
Wheelbase 56.5in (1435mm)
Weight 235lb (107kg)
Top speed 45mph (72kph)
Price $210 (battery), $250 (magneto)

The "clutch" lever shown here featured a sping-loaded thumb release and notches on the gate to ensure constant tension on the leather drive belt.

(battery or magneto) with 26-inch (66cm) wheels for shorter-legged riders.

The engine was slightly more powerful. With bore and stroke of 3.31 x 3.5 inches (84 x 89mm), displacement was up to 30.16 cubic inches (494cc) and a rating of 4.3 horsepower. Top speed was about 45mph (72kph).

The big, if not necessarily good, news was the arrival of the much anticipated V-twin. The 45-degree inline twin was built on a beefed-up bottom end, with the magneto gear-driven off the crankshaft. The 3 x 3.5 inch (76 x 89mm) bore and stroke put displacement at 49 cubic

inches (810cc). Rated at 7 horsepower, the 5D was reportedly good for 65mph (105kph).

But at the price of $325, with no drive belt tensioner, the new twin didn't perform as Milwaukee had hoped. The engine was not easy to start, and the atmospheric inlet valves were at odds with the crankcase pressures of a V-twin. Only 27 of the twins were built, of which only two are known to remain in existence today.

The battery-equipped single accounted for the bulk of production in 1909, with

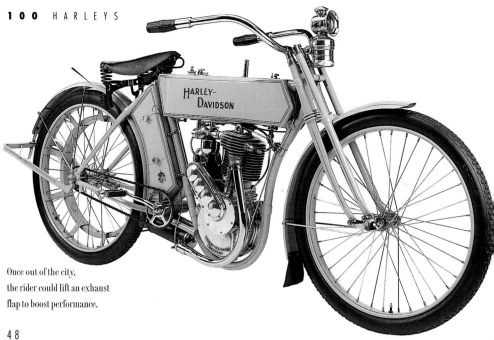

Once out of the city,
the rider could lift an exhaust
flap to boost performance.

more than 1,030 manufactured. The factory produced only 90 singles fitted with the magneto.

Linkage control rods for the throttle and spark advance had been replaced by wires routed through the handlebars. The oil tank was no longer strapped above the fuel tank. The new twin backbone frame carried a single tank with shared compartments; 1.5 gallons (5.7lit) for fuel and 2 quarts (1.9lit) of oil. The oil was delivered to the engine with a drip-feed line. Wheelbase, as a result of development on the twin, had grown to 56.5 inches (1435mm).

The Milwaukee motorcycles also received new styling touches in 1909. The longer fuel tank was formed in two halves, which tapered at both ends, and fitted flush with the rear downtube. The space between the rear fender and frame held a fitted compartment for tools, parts and riding accessories. The color choices remained renault gray or piano finish black.

The diagonal cover houses four gears carrying power from the crankshaft to the magneto.

Model 7D **1911**

The singles went largely unchanged in 1910, but for the addition of an idler arm, allowing the rider to let the engine idle without disengaging the belt. Black paint was no longer offered, so all the Silent Gray Fellows were now gray. The V-twin was absent from the line, undergoing redesign in anticipation of its re-appearance in 1911.

But despite Milwaukee's disappointment with the results of its first twin, the overall picture for 1910 was hardly grim. The factory had grown to nearly 10,000 square feet (930m²), 149 workers were employed and production nearly tripled.

In four years there had been no increases in price. But in 1910, for the first time, a special model appeared on the roster. The 6E stock racer was priced at $275. A few 6E models, prototypes of the revised twin, were sold to bona fide racing customers.

However, the V-twin was back in 1911. Displacement remained at 49ci (810cc), but the new engine featured mechanical intake valves and a belt

MODEL 7D 1911

Engine IOE 45° V-twin
Displacement 49.48ci (810cc)
Transmission Direct drive
Horsepower 6.5
Wheelbase 56.5in (1435mm)
Weight 295lb (134kg)
Top speed 60mph (97kph)
Price $300

Vertical fins on the cylinder heads provided better engine cooling. The magneto was now situated behind the cylinders.

tensioner. Horsepower was rated at 6.5, just over two more ponies than the single. The cylinder heads on both singles and twins now had vertical rather than horizontal finning. The new twin's frame was reinforced and slightly lower than the original, and the front downtube was now straight on both the single and twin. Frames and bodywork remained gray, but broad striping in red or dark gray had replaced the pin stripes of earlier years.

Production numbers for 1911 are missing from the factory archives. Some early records were destroyed by a flood.

Historian Jerry Hatfield quotes records that put total production for 1911 as 5,625. How many were V-twins is unknown.

It is known that the new twin, designated 7D, was a considerable improvement over the 1909 version. The motorcycle was stronger, lower, more powerful, ran smoother and handled better. But the price was daunting at $300. Buyers could choose from a number of established twins with more displacement for less money, or from several four-cylinder marques. Competition in the marketplace was stiff.

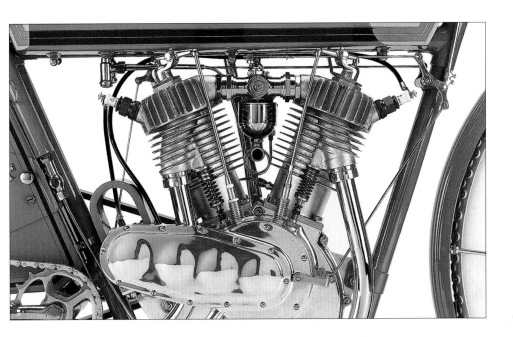

Model X8E **1912**

P rompted by Indian's racing success, the factory made numerous improvements to the motorcycles for 1912. The new Harley-Davidson frame was lower, the result of shortening the rear down-tube and angling the top crosstube forward of the seat. This put the rider closer to the center of the machine, with an easier reach to the handlebars. Comfort was further enhanced by the intoduction of the Ful-

Floteing Seat, and with it the advent of Kute Speling. The frame's rear downtube was fitted with a long spring below the seat post. The saddle itself was still sprung, but now the whole assembly had four inches (10cm) of suspension travel. The new chassis enhanced not only the roadholding capabilities of the machine, but also the likelihood the rider would stay attached to it at speed.

And speeds were up, because the V-twin was now offered in a 60.32 cubic-inch (989cc) version with close to eight horsepower. This E model was $10 more than the standard 6.5-horsepower

MODEL X8E 1912

Engine IOE 45° V-twin
Displacement 60.32ci (989cc)
Transmission Direct drive
Horsepower 8
Wheelbase 56.5in (1435mm)
Weight 312lb (141.5kg)
Top speed 65mph (105kph)
Price $285

RIGHT: Detail of one of the spark plugs.
FAR RIGHT: The 1912 twin featured a slotted gear on the left side of the crankshaft which admitted oil to the primary chain.

twin, but with it came Harley-Davidson's first clutch. "Free wheel control," developed by William Harley and associate Henry Melk, was a rear wheel hub-mounted clutch operated by a left-side hand lever. (The letter "X" in the model names indicated the provision of a clutch.) And, for the first time in Harley history, the customer had his choice of belt (8D and X8D) or chain drive (X8E).

Nor was that all. The pedal cranks were fitted with eccentric discs in the frame, so the chain on the pedal crank could be adjusted independent of the drive chain or belt. Meaning no need to move the rear wheel.

Also, the big twin engine was Harley's first with self-aligning ball bearings on the crankshaft and roller bearings supporting the connecting rods. The

ABOVE: The lever adjacent to the tank operated Harley-Davidson's first clutch, located in the rear wheel hub.

engine also featured a crankcase breather that incorporated an oiler for the primary chain. The signs of High Performance were now showing in Milwaukee. And the style of the motorcycle was evolving as well. The fuel tank complemented the lower slung frame and the fenders grew skirts. The first – albeit slight – hints of streamlining were beginning to appear.

The single's intake valve
was operated by a pushrod
from the timing case.

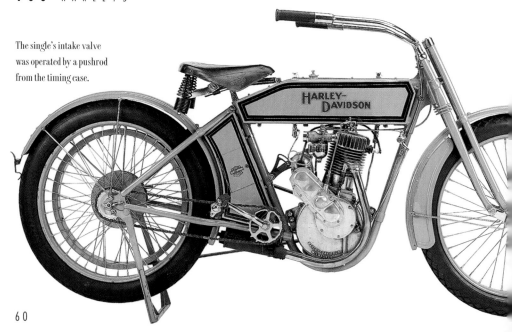

Model 9 **1913**

Although the new V-twin outsold the single in 1912, the less expensive thumper still figured strongly in the motoring mix. Prosperity or not, not everyone could afford the big bike, and the single remained trustworthy and serviceable. And it was larger. For 1913 Harley-Davidson announced what would come to be called the "5-35" motor; 5 horsepower and 35 cubic inches (565cc). The price was up to $290, for belt (9A) or chain drive (9B), which was $60 less than the V-twin (9E).

Of course the single had benefited from the development work devoted to its big brother. Mechanically operated intake valve, lighter alloy piston and improved carburetion were included in the package. And the flywheel, rod and piston were balanced as an assembly.

The color choice remained gray, and all models were fitted with 28 x 2.75-inch tires. The single still carried its oil supply in a compartment in the fuel tank. The bicycle pedals remained, but the single now featured the rear hub clutch.

MODEL 9A 1913

Engine IOE single
Displacement 34.47ci (595cc)
Transmission Direct drive
Horsepower 4.5
Wheelbase 56.5in (1435mm)
Weight 316lb (143kg)
Top speed 50mph (80kph)
Price $290

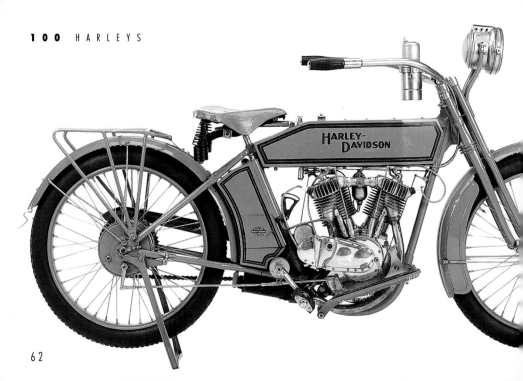

Model 10F 1914

Motorcycle technology Milwaukee-style took several more leaps in 1914. Two-speed transmissions, step-starters, footboards, enclosed valve springs and primary chains, and sidecars all debuted as the popularity of motorcycling boomed. Harley Davidson enjoyed a considerable measure of this mushrooming market, but was forced to share it with at least three other entrepreneurs of the age.

They were George Hendee at Indian, Ignatz Schwinn of Excelesior, and the Henderson brothers, who built Ace Motorcycles. And there was one other motoring mogul in rapid rise at the time, Henry Ford.

Automobiles, like motorcycles, were still hand-made, but the advent of moving assembly lines boosted car production enormously. The mass production of motorcycles would be forever limited by the affordability of cars, and two-wheelers began the shift to sport and recreational machines rather than primary transportation. The competition

MODEL 10F 1914

Engine IOE 45° V-twin
Displacement 60.33ci (988cc)
Transmission Two-speed
Horsepower 11
Wheelbase 56.5in (1435mm)
Weight 310lb (141kg)
Top speed 65mph (105kph)
Price $285

RIGHT: 1914 was a time of technological advance. A two-speed rear hub was introduced, as was a step-starter and footboards. The V-twin engine featured enclosed valve springs.

for a market share of the smaller pie had grown intense.

Despite its reputation for sturdy equipment and reliable performance, Harley-Davidson was losing the public popularity contest generated by motorcycle racing. If the machines were to be cast forever in the sporting mode, then the successful builder was obliged to meet the requirements of the sporting rider. At the same time, the Milwaukee faction knew that the touring and Sunday-putt riders would always outnumber the young daredevils. So the task was to provide motorcycles for both.

The combined appeals of horsepower and operating ease were addressed differently by the industry leaders. The contest pitted the V-twins of Indian and Harley-Davidson against the inline fours from Henderson, which was based at this time in Detroit. The four was smooth and powerful, but more expensive to manufacture and maintain. The V-twins were less smooth but reliable, and acquitted themselves well in uses where top speed mattered little. Economics would eventually decide in the twins' favor, but the fours remained an option into the late 1920s.

Model 11J **1915**

MODEL 11J 1915

Engine IOE 45° V-twin
Displacement 60.33ci
(988cc)
Transmission Three-speed
Horsepower 11
Wheelbase 59.5in
(1511mm)
Weight 325lb (147kg)
Top speed 60mph
(97kph)
Price $310

Milwaukee had shown in 1914 that it was ready and able to build modern motorcycles. In 1915 Harley-Davidson not only quickened the pace of improvement, but also displayed its new commitment to professional racing.

The most significant advance for road and track was the introduction of a three-speed transmission. The sliding-gear mechanism provided attachment of the step-starter to the gearbox. With transmission and clutch fitted amidships, the 11J certified Harley's position in the mainstream of American motorcycle manufacturing. It was also the first model equipped with an electric headlight.

At $310, the J model carried a hefty price tag. The 60-inch twin (989cc) with magneto was offered at $240 for the single-speed version (11E) and $275 for the three-speed (11F). Two singles remained in the catalog, the one speed B and two-speed C models at $200 and $230 respectively. The racing K model ("stripped stock") was priced at $250.

1915 saw the introduction of three-speed transmission.

Model 16J **1916**

MODEL 16J 1916

Engine IOE 45° V-twin
Displacement 60.33ci
(988cc)
Transmission Three-speed
Horsepower 11 @
3000rpm
Wheelbase 59.5in
(1511mm)
Weight 325lb (147kg)
Top speed 60mph
(97kph)
Price $295

Racing would provide Milwaukee with substantial bragging rights in 1915. Following the factory team's marginal success the preceding season, Bill Harley and William Ottaway brought new determination, and equipment, to the line for the following year. Of the 17 models now offered in the catalog, eight were racing bikes.

The sidecar also took on new stature in 1915. A new chassis and longer body replaced the original model, and advertising emphasized the economic benefits of sidecar travel. The chairs or sidehacks as they came to be called,

In 1916 the frame was
reinforced for sidecar use,
and the steering
head bearings were
enlarged.

also found wide application in the postal and military services. The early sidecar bodies were built by the Seaman Company in Milwaukee. Right-side chairs were designed for the U.S. and Europe, while left-side rigs were fitted for the British market.

One requirement shared by racers and sidecarists was the need for more power. Harley-Davidson advertised a guaranteed 11 horsepower from the 61-inch V-twin, noting that dynamometer readings had been as high as 16 horsepower. The racing engines were said to be making nearly 20.

These increases were largely the result of better intake and exhaust design, with larger ports, valves and carburetors. Beefier flywheels, rod bearings, and crank-pins were designed so as to handle the higher horsepower. And the engineering efforts were certified on the race track.

In 1916 Harley-Davidson introduced its step-starter and dispensed with the last major bicycle component. The

ABOVE: The Prest-O-Lite acetylene tank for the lights was mounted at the bottom rear of the sidecar

RIGHT: The fuel tank on the '16 was more rounded than its counterpart of a year earlier.

pedals were gone, at least on the twins with gearboxes. The model numbering system was also changed, brought up to date by using the current year as the prefix. Engineering changes included stronger frames that were common to singles and twins. Both were available with either direct drive or the three-speed transmission. The basic twin with magneto sold for $240, while the gear-selecting version with battery and lights went for $295. The single-speed single was $200 and another $30 was added for the three-speed.

Functional development resulted in styling shifts as well. The larger fuel tank and fenders featured more rounded shapes, as the first hints of streamlining appeared from Milwaukee. Harley's characteristic prudence in product development was to serve the company well.

8-Valve Racer 1916-23

Indian had introduced its 8-valve racing machine in 1912, and offered it for public sale at little more than the conventional road model. The Federation of American Motorcyclists (F.A.M.), in the interest of ensuring a level playing field, stipulated that manufacturers must offer their racers for public sale. But they said nothing about price. So Milwaukee priced the new 8-valve at $1,500 to discourage privateers, and it worked. No record has been turned up showing civilian ownership of a Harley 8-valve until after the factory team was dissolved.

Just how many of the 8-valves were built is unknown. Even among expert historians and restorers there is wide disagreement; some say as few as ten were built, others say it was more like 50. A number of engines were sent to England, Europe and Australia, and some machines were converted to singles. Since the 8-valve was still available as late as 1928, an educated

8-VALVE RACER 1916-23

Engine Overhead-valve 45° V-twin
Displacement 60.33ci (988cc)
Transmission Direct drive
Horsepower c.14-16
Wheelbase 51.5in (1308mm)
Weight 275lb (125kg)
Top speed 115mph (185kph)
Price $1,500

FIRST AT OMAHA

Otto Ranier, riding his stock Harley-Davidson twin, took first place in each of the four events he entered at Omaha, July 4th.

The races were held over a course laid out from Florence to Fifty-second and Dodge Streets.

According to Omaha newspapers young Ranier clinched hills like a streak and outraced his competitors by thirty feet at every goal.

In two events Mark Schwerin finished second, also riding a Harley-Davidson.

HARLEY-DAVIDSON MOTOR COMPANY
Producers of High-Grade Motorcycles for More Than Twelve Years
Milwaukee, Wis., U. S. A.

RIGHT: The 90-degree valve angle and hemispherical combustion chambers followed aircraft engine design principles.

guess puts the total somewhere between 30 and 50 bikes.

According to the company history, the first three overhead-valve racers were built in 1916. One had a manual oil pump, one a mechanical pump and the third was fitted with one each. The machines were relatively short-coupled, with wheelbase at about 50 inches (1270mm). The bikes had a keystone frame, with front and rear downtubes bolted to plates attached to the engine, making it a stressed member.

These engines made good power, probably close to 20 when the weather was right. Compression ratios were elevated considerably, and starting procedures usually required a tow rope and a car. It wasn't long before these machines were averaging over 100mph (161kph) on the board tracks. By then the pocket-valve engines were only a few ticks slower, and often carried the day when the 8-valves expired from fried valves, seizures or fractured engine components.

Harley-Davidson advertised the 8-valve ($1,500) and the 4-valve single ($1,400) as a gesture of compliance with the F.A.M. edict.

Model 17J **1917**

The early '17 models were the last of the Silent Gray Fellows as World War I brought the advent of the Silent Green Soldiers, or the Olive Drab Doughboys.

From the Harley-Davidson brochure: "It is a really strange coincidence that within recent years various governments of the world have selected this color as the most serviceable for government equipment such as motorcycles, automobiles and motor trucks. The new military drab color furnishes a most delightful contrast with the handsome satin nickel finish used on many of the motor parts." Olive green would become Milwaukee's standard color for years beyond the military conflict. But for a brief interlude of darker brewster green in the early 1920s, Harley-Davidson stretched its supply of olive green paint until the advent of the 1932 model year.

In 1917 the V-twin inherited the four-lobe cam designed for the 8-valve racer. Valve lift and timing were revised for the

MODEL J 1917

Engine IOE 45° V-twin
Displacement 60.33ci (988cc)
Transmission Three-speed
Horsepower 16 @ 3000rpm
Wheelbase 59.5in (1511mm)
Weight 325lb (147kg)
Top speed 65mph (105kph)
Price $310

RIGHT: A speedometer was an extra-cost accessory. The top needle remained on the highest speed attained.

FAR RIGHT: The war eliminated the supply of Bosch magnetos, which were replaced by Dixie units.

demands of increased performance. The gear-driven oil pump, introduced in 1915, ensured that lubrication was delivered in proper amounts to the critical moving parts. The earlier hand pump and drip-feed oiling systems often created either a shortage or surplus of oil in the engine, both of which meant problems.

For sidecar use, Milwaukee recommended the 14-tooth countershaft sprocket for a higher gear ratio. The order blank noted: "This motor develops slightly less speed but gives maximum efficiency where power is needed.

This motor can also be used satisfactorily for solo riding."

The sidecar enjoyed its highest popularity in this heady era that created rural mail delivery and mechanized warfare. Although Indian was the primary supplier of military motorcycles during World War I, Milwaukee provided its share of motorcycles with sidecars rigged for combat. The sidecar for civilian use sold for $80.

By this point the V-twin's popularity had limited the single to mostly commercial and racing applications. Of the 18,522 motorcycles built by Harley-Davidson for 1917, only about 730 were singles. But Milwaukee had noted the demand for a lightweight sporting machine, and concluded that a smaller twin would be the logical choice. So work began on the Sport Model W that would appear in 1919.

LEFT: Firestone Tires put their advertising where the rubber meets the road. FAR LEFT: The intake valve springs were enclosed in 1917, and valve timing on the intake side was revised for more power.

Model W Sport Twin **1919**

**MODEL W SPORT TWIN
1919**

Engine Flathead
opposed twin
Displacement 35.64ci
(584cc)
Transmission Unit
three-speed
Horsepower 6
Wheelbase 57in
(1448mm)
Weight 265lb (120kg)
Top speed 50mph (80kph)
Price $335

As American motorcycling shifted focus after the war from transportation to recreation mode, the interest in lightweight sport bikes rose accordingly. Harley-Davidson responded with the Model W Sport Twin, a 36ci (584cc) horizontally opposed twin featuring an integral three-speed transmission.

Set lengthwise and low in the frame, the flathead boxer engine had a large external flywheel and an enclosed drive chain. Given the nearly perfect primary balance factor of this engine design, the Sport Twin was by far the smoothest running Harley-Davidson ever built, past or present. The motor, rated at a meager 6 horsepower, was comfortably understressed and the motorcycle weighed only 265 pounds (120kg). Patterned after the British Douglas, the W model was a radical departure for Harley-Davidson in terms of design and engineering. The chassis incorporated a keystone frame, utilizing the engine as a stressed member. While that feature was familiar on the 8-valve racer, everything else about

the Sport Model was different from the well-established line of V-twins.

The intake and exhaust manifolds were long, siamesed tubes along the right side of the engine. The prevailing notion held that preheating the intake charge enhanced the combustion process. A single camshaft operated all four valves. The screw-in valve guides were easily accessible for replacement, and the valves could be removed without pulling the engine. The cylinders and heads were still a single casting, but they could also be detached without removing the engine.

Ease of maintenance and the accessibility of components had played a role in the motorcycle's design.

Roller bearings supported both the crankshaft and connecting rods, and the geared primary drove the wet clutch and magneto mounted atop the engine. The early models came with magnetos and with or without acetylene lights. From 1921 through its final year in 1923, the Sport Twin was offered with either magneto ignition (WF) or battery (WJ).

The sporty twin also incorporated a fork unlike other Harley models. The trailing lower links connected by rods to

LEFT: The horizontally opposed Sport Twin was unlike any Harley-Davidson before or since. Though advanced in many respects, the lightweight sport model achieved little success in the U.S.

RIGHT: "Roaring into the Twenties," a pewter commemorative plate issued in a limited edition of 3,000 by Harley-Davidson in 1994.

upper links acting on a central spring. The fender, attached to the Merkel-style truss fork, was stationary as the front wheel moved up and down. Rear suspension was absent save the enclosed springs beneath the solo saddle. The fuel tank, which carried 2.75 gallons (10.4lit) of gas and two quarts (1.9lit) of oil, was situated between the upper frame tubes. The rear luggage rack was standard equipment.

Despite its shortage of both horsepower and ground clearance, the Sport Twin was a record-setting machine. Hap Scherer set a winning time in the 3-Flags run from Canada to Mexico, and the WJ was the first motorcycle to ascend Mt. Baldy.

Unfortunately these victories had little effect on the Sport's popularity. The V-twin had been firmly established as the American motorcycle engine of choice, whether in medium, large or extra large. Utilitarian twins of non-V configuration were met with general disinterest in the United States.

The single casting
intake/exhaust manifold
was something of a
curiosity.

Model J **1921**

The first Harley-Davidson J model was sold in 1915. The letter designation was applied to both the first three-speed twin and the premier model with "complete electrical equipment." Proven on road and track, in peace and war, the J model became Milwaukee's top-of-the-line motorcycle.

In 1921 the 61-inch twin (1000cc) was joined by a bigger brother, the 74-inch (1200cc) JD (battery) and FD (magneto). Rated by the factory at 18 horsepower, the big twin was touted as the ideal mate to the new two-passenger sidecar. The sidecar motor (JDS) was fitted with compression shims for the lower rpm chores imposed by the chair. It also had a 16-tooth countershaft sprocket, two teeth fewer than the solo motor.

Development of the JD was prompted by the growing popularity of four-cylinder engines from Indian, Henderson and Cleveland. Smoother, more powerful fours threatened to dilute the dominance of V-twins in the sporting, commercial and police markets. Milwaukee had considered building a four, but eventually

MODEL J 1921

Engine IOE 45° V-twin
Displacement 74.66ci (1207cc)
Transmission Three-speed
Horsepower 18 @ 3000rpm
Wheelbase 59.5in (1511mm)
Weight 365lb (166kg)
Top speed 70mph (113kph)
Price $485

RIGHT: The J model
(Sixty-one) could be
simply distinguished from
the JD (Seventy-four)
by the five, rather than
six, cylinder fins above
the exhaust port.

rejected the idea in favor of upgrading the V-twin. And the decision proved out.

Of course the record doesn't show whether or not the co-founders could predict the future. But 1921 was a disastrous year for sales. Government contracts during the war had accelerated production, and Harley-Davidson registered a record year of more than 27,000 machines in 1920. With surplus inventory on hand, production for 1921 dropped to 11,460.

But the war had stimulated engineering and production improvements, due largely to research and development on aircraft engines. As these advances filtered down to automobile and motorcycle production lines, the engines showed gains in efficiency, power and durability. So even as engine technology made significant strides, the overall market was in decline. And not only was the flat economy to blame; two other factors put motorcycles at a disadvantage. Henry Ford had again lowered the prices on his cars, and motorcycling was once more facing a problem as hell-raising hot rodders damaged the image of motorcycling in the eyes of the public.

Model JD **1926**

MODEL JD 1926

Engine IOE 45° V-twin
Displacement 74.66ci
(1207cc)
Transmission Three-speed
Horsepower 24
Wheelbase 59.5in
(1511mm)
Weight 405lb (184kg)
Top speed 60mph
(97kph)
Price $335

For the first 20 years in Harley-Davidson's existence, engineering had the dominant role in motorcycle design. With the mid-1920s came a new emphasis on styling. For 1922 and '23, the traditional olive green paint was replaced by darker brewster green with gold striping. Olive remained available as an optional color, and returned as the standard hue in 1924. In 1926 Milwaukee offered white and cream as color options.

The flagging motorcycle market had stimulated action on several fronts in Milwaukee. Advertising and public relations efforts were stepped up, the designers and engineers made advances in engine efficiency, suspension and ease of maintenance for the rider. For 1924 the twins featured grease fittings on the running gear, stronger front forks, iron-alloy pistons, new exhaust pipes, larger batteries and generators. Late in the year the two-cam got a new valve train design that brought increased power. While streamlined styling and direct mail campaigns were

The first "Stream-Line"
models appeared in 1925.
The teardrop shape of the
fuel tank followed
contemporary styling.

employed to attract new buyers, the design and construction of these new models were intended to impress riders by offering higher standards of performance and reliability. In 1925 the cradle frame was replaced by a lower unit using an engine plate between the front and rear downtubes. Seat height was reduced by three inches (7.62cm), which provided a lower center of gravity and easier handling.

Smaller diameter wheel rims also contributed to the lower overall stance, and wider tires provided better grip on the roadway. With softer front suspension, and shorter handlebars with a slight downward bend, the new twins handled significantly better than their predecessors. The more forward seat position put the rider in better control of the machine, and the seat-post spring had been lengthened from 9 to 14 inches (22.9 to 35.6cm).

What's more, Milwaukee had dropped the price of the Sixty-ones by five dollars. And the Seventy-fours were offered at the previous year's prices, despite the fact that the new models represented considerable investment in design, engineering, tooling and parts.

A pewter miniature model of a 1922 JD that was produced in 1993. These small sculptures are desktop favorites among Harley fans.

The electrically equipped
B model cost $25 more than
the magneto version.

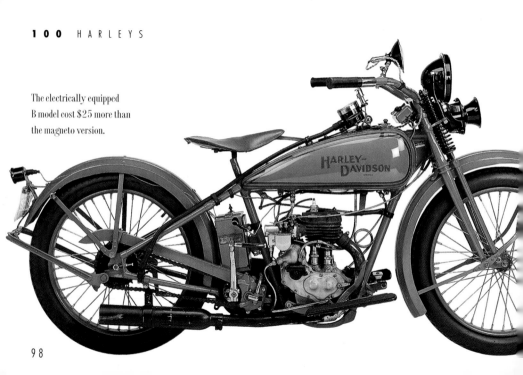

Models A & B **1926**

Despite the slow market in the mid-1920s, Harley-Davidson was obviously intent on maintaining its hard-won position of leadership in the motorcycle industry.

Milwaukee had gone without a road model single for three years, but with the advent of Indian's 21-inch (350cc) Prince in 1925, Harley-Davidson reacted quickly with two singles the following year. The 350s marked Harley's first side-valve engine since the Sport Twin, and the first overhead-valve powerplant offered to the public (in

the form of the AA and BA models). The ohv version actually debuted in 1925 at a Milwaukee race, and was soon dubbed the Peashooter for its staccato exhaust note. The ohv engine was built in limited numbers and primarily for racing.

The A (magneto) and B (battery) side-valve models accounted for more than 7,000 machines, most of which were exported to Great Britain, Europe and Australia. The single had a three-speed transmission, "ful-floeting" seat and external contracting rear brake. And it sold for $210, $50 less than its pocket-valve predecessor of 1918.

MODEL A 1926

Engine Side-valve single
Displacement 21.1ci (346cc)
Transmission Three-speed
Horsepower 8
Wheelbase 56.5in (1435mm)
Weight 251lb (114kg)
Top speed 55mph (88kph)
Price $210

Model BA **1927**

Harley-Davidson's first experience with side-valve engines, more commonly known as flatheads, was not hugely successful. The Sport Twin did not sell well in the U.S.A., losing out to the popular Indian Sport Scout, a 45-inch (750cc) V-twin. But Milwaukee hadn't lost interest in the design.

Economic realities, in both commercial and sporting contexts, had perpetuated the market for less expensive mounts. Harley and Indian both built and maintained a brace of racing thumpers in the 1920s, as the big-inch twins slowly dissolved into racing history. Thus it was decided that two singles would be developed simultaneously; a side-valve model for economical transportation and an overhead-valve version for sport riders and racers. Naturally the flatheads, models A (magneto) and B (battery), were produced in far greater numbers. Rated at 8 horsepower, the side-valves sold for $210 and $235 respectively. The 12-horsepower overheads (AA and BA) were $250 and $275. The racing model (S) was priced at $300.

MODEL BA 1927

Engine Overhead-valve single

Displacement 21.1ci (346cc)

Transmission Three-speed

Horsepower 12

Wheelbase 56.5in (1435mm)

Weight 263lb (119kg)

Top speed 60mph (97kph)

Price $275

ABOVE: The shift lever on the left of the tank operated the gearbox.

Unlike the twins, the new singles featured detachable cylinder heads. The combustion chambers, pioneered and patented by British engineer Harry Ricardo, incorporated what came to be called a "squish band." The design created turbulence in the fuel charge, which translated as more complete combustion and higher horsepower. In racing trim, the Peashooter weighed about 235 pounds (106.6kg) and could reach upwards of 70mph (113kph).

Harley-Davidson won six of the 14 national championship 350cc races in 1926, with Indian victorious in the remaining eight.

So the singles appealed to that steadfast, but more or less static segment of the motorcycling fraternity that prized lightweight sport bikes, and their budget-minded counterparts who simply couldn't afford a twin. And while their numbers, at least in the United States, were relatively small, the complementary considerations of sport riding and economic utility ensured them some choice of equipment.

103

Model JDH **1929**

K nown as the Two-Cam, the JDH made its first appearance in 1928, and it was offered in both JH and JDH models, respectively 61 and 74 cubic inch (1000cc and 1200cc) versions. This engine was derived from Milwaukee's racing experience gleaned throughout the 1920s.

Prompted by the improving performance figures of the Indian Powerplus and the four-cylinder Excelsior, Harley needed a faster machine. The factory had built many twin-cam competition bikes, and simply decided to apply that knowledge to the production of a road model. So the JDH got the racer's direct valve gear, with tappets replacing the standard roller arms. Adding dual intake valve springs, the Two-Cam was capable of higher rpm. Larger cooling fins on the cylinder head helped dissipate the heat inevitably created by more power, and a new throttle-controlled oil pump improved engine lubrication.

The Two-Cam was equipped with domed Dow metal pistons, optional on the J and JD, manufactured with magnesium alloy. This meant higher compression.

MODEL JDH 1929

Engine IOE 45° V-twin
Displacement 74.66ci (1207cc)
Transmission Three-speed
Horsepower 29 @ 4000rpm
Wheelbase 59.5in (1511mm)
Weight 408lb (185kg)
Top speed 85mph (137kph)
Price $370

ABOVE: Ammeter flanked by ignition and light switches. RIGHT: Large cooling fins help dissipate engine heat.

The JDH had a smaller and lighter fuel tank than the standard road machines, with capacity reduced from 5.3 to 4.75 gallons (20 to 18lit). Smaller diameter wheels lowered the center of gravity, and heavy duty spokes in the rear wheel helped handle the additional power. With more speed, the addition of a front brake was welcomed by sport riders.

But 1929, at the edge of the Great Depression, would be the final year for the J series. Some 75,000 of the bikes had been built in its nine-year run, and it had evolved as the ultimate logical extension of its progenitor, the 1911 V-twin. In that time the horsepower had risen, the electrics acquired dependability, the styling had achieved acceptance and the motorcycle ranked well for overall performance and reliability. But other forces were at play in the market. Reality intervened, in the form of the Great Depression, and with it the fact that flatheads could be produced more cheaply. Nonetheless, the JDH had set the pattern for the next high-performance Harley, the 1936 ohv Knucklehead. The Roaring Twenties had to end, but when they did the JD had established itself as the pioneer Hog.

Model DL **1929**

As years go, 1929 is rarely recalled as one of America's best. But although the collapse of the stock market has become the signal event in history, the first nine months of the year looked encouraging in Milwaukee.

Two new models appeared in 1929; the 45 cubic inch (750cc) V-twin D (standard) and DL (high compression) model and the 30.50 inch (500cc) model C single. Neither of them looked too appealing

to riders accustomed to 1000 and 1200cc twins, but those models were still available. At $255, the new single was $115 cheaper than the JDH, and the 45-inch (750cc) twin only cost $290. Riders unable to afford a big twin now at least had the benefit of more economical mounts from Milwaukee.

Indian had been achieving notable performance with their flathead V-twins. Harley-Davidson was stung when Indian captured all the national championship races in 1928, a feat they repeated in 1929. Indian had proven the reliabilty and performance of flatheads in 750,

MODEL DL 1929

Engine Side-valve 45°
V-twin
Displacement 45.32ci
(746cc)
Transmission Three-speed
Horsepower 18.5 @
4000rpm
Wheelbase 57.5in
(1460mm)
Weight 390lb (177kg)
Top speed 70mph
(113kph)
Price $290

1000 and 1200cc engines. So it was obvious in Milwaukee than something more than just a mildly-tuned flathead for the road was in order.

But the smaller V-twin had never been intended as a high performance motorcycle. Practical, economical transportation was its role, and reliable service in commercial applications. Nonetheless, William Ottaway was already at work on a more powerful

version of the D model (with overhead valves), and plans were well underway for big twins of the flathead persuasion. Milwaukee had faced the facts: the side-valve made sufficient power for the open road, it was a quieter engine by design, and it was less expensive to build than its ohv counterpart. In 1930 the "small twin" got a new frame and front fork, and a sport model (DLD) was introduced that featured higher compression.

The DL Sport Solo
was the high
compression version
of the 45-inch (746cc)
flathead V-twin.

Model C **1930**

The Model C, a new single-cylinder machine of 30.5 cubic inch (500cc) displacement which used the same frame as the 45-inch Model D, was introduced in 1930.

The singles followed a similar line of development to the Forty-five V-twins. Even though sales of the Twenty-one had declined for several years, Milwaukee thought a bigger single was in order. Thus the C model, a 30.50 cubic inch (500cc) single which shared the same frame with the 350 single and 750 twin.

The 500cc single, known in the U.S. as the Thirty-fifty, became the only single in Milwaukee's lineup for 1931. Even though Joe Petrali was blitzing the race tracks on the 21-inch (350cc) Peashooter, the overwhelming effects of the Depression were felt throughout

MODEL C 1930

Engine Side-valve single
Displacement 30.1ci (493cc)
Transmission Three-speed
Horsepower 10.4 @ 3600rpm
Wheelbase 57.5in (1460mm)
Weight 340lb (154kg)
Top speed 60mph (97kph)
Price $260

the country. Most people simply couldn't afford a motorcycle. In 1932 Harley-Davidson again offered the 350 single, dropping the price to $195, the lowest tag ever on a Milwaukee machine. The 30.50in (500cc) single was reduced to $235, the price of a 350 only three years earlier.

As Europe likewise fell into economic doldrums, and import tariffs rose, Milwaukee's export markets shriveled

up. The days of the economic and/or sporty singles were numbered, and 1934 would be their last year of production. The national championship racing class for 350s (Class A) carried on for several years, and in 1935 Joe Petrali won every meet on the calendar. A few years later the Class C formula, for 750cc flatheads, became the standardized format for American racing.

At $260, the Model C was
one of Milwaukee's more
economical mounts.

Model VL **1930**

MODEL VL 1930

Engine Side-valve 45°
V-twin
Displacement 73.73ci
(1208cc)
Transmission Three-speed
Horsepower 30 @
4000rpm
Wheelbase 60in
(1524mm)
Weight 529lb (240kg)
Top speed 85mph
(137kph)
Price $340

The new 74 had appeared in mid-1929, little more than two months before the stock market disintegrated. Though they were still called Seventy-fours, the 1930 V (standard) and VL (high compression) models were entirely different motorcycles from the earlier FD and JD models. And at first it was not the machine Milwaukee had hoped for.

The VL did produce a tad more horsepower than the JD, and featured a new frame and fork. But it was less than reliable. At $340, twenty bucks more than the JD, the VL had a weak clutch, frail flywheel, poor lubrication, bad valve

springs, inefficient mufflers and marginal pistons. Otherwise it was just fine.

Fans of the JD, especially high-performance adherents of the JDH, scoffed at the new flathead. To them it seemed a step backwards, a pedestrian design in a package more than 100 pounds (45kg) heavier than its predecessor. But the performance figures were nearly identical, and Milwaukee moved quickly to correct the deficiencies revealed in the early models. Moreover, the VL added features such as

RIGHT: The sidecar had gone largely unchanged for a decade. All three wheels were now interchangeable and the sidecar had a brake integrated with the motorcycle's stoppers.

detachable cylinder heads, interchangeable wheels, bigger brakes and tires, lower seat height and more ground clearance. And a wider torque spread than the J motor offered.

Harley-Davidson had built the flathead big twin to contend with the Indian Chief, which had a similar configuration. So the future, at least that foreseeable portion, was a side-valve vision. The standard V model made 28 horsepower, while the higher compression VL cranked out 30. Like the Forty-five, each valve had its own cam and the lubrication system remained total-loss. A forged I-beam front fork replaced the tube-style of the J model. New 19-inch wheels came standard with 4.00-inch tires and 4.40-inch rubber was an extra cost option.

Four versions of the new Seventy-four were available in 1930: the V and VL with batteries and the VM and VLM each with a magneto-generator. The battery was a stouter 22-amp unit and the coil was better sealed against the elements. The tool box was still a cylinder fitted below the "Clear-the-way Horn" and "Two Bullet Headlights". In 1931 the tool container became an oval shape with a new disk-type horn on its front.

Model VLD 1934

The VLD Special Sport Solo was introduced in 1933. The full force of the Great Depression had reached Milwaukee in 1931, and production had dropped to the lowest figure in 20 years. In the two years that followed, the picture grew even worse.

At Harley-Davidson, with management and labor alike working for reduced rates of pay, technological advancement was not on the agenda. So color and graphics took on new importance. Following the lead of the automobile industry, Milwaukee introduced Art Deco styling to the motorcycles. The 1933 fuel tanks featured a stylized eagle in flight, accented by gold stripes and contrasting colors. The design, a variation on optional scrollwork on 1932 tanks, was used for only one year.

Not that the new models were simply old machines in colorful garb. Numerous improvements developed before the economic crisis had been incorporated a year earlier.

MODEL VLD 1934

Engine Side-valve 45° V-twin
Displacement 73.73ci (1208cc)
Transmission Three-speed
Horsepower 36 @ 4500rpm
Wheelbase 60in (1524mm)
Weight 529lb (240kg)
Top speed 85mph (137kph)
Price $310

121

More streamlined fenders
reflect the design
influence of Art Deco
in the 1930s.

The V series had new cylinders, designed for better heat dissipation, plus an improved oil pump, new generator and stronger fork. The same upgrades appeared on the Forty-fives, now called the R series, and the Thirty-fifty singles.

The VLD was to the big twin flatheads what the JDH had been to the earlier 74, the factory hot rod. A new Y-shaped intake manifold gave the fuel charge a more direct shot into the cylinders, and a new Linkert die-cast brass carburetor was fitted. With aluminum alloy pistons replacing magnesium alloy, new cylinder heads and a compression ratio of 5:1, the engine made 36 horsepower at 4500rpm. Acceleration, given the machine's weight, was robust.

In 1934 the V and R series were fitted with skirted rear fenders and upswept exhaust tips. For 1934 the fishtail muffler returned on the twins, and the 74 toolbox was changed to a box fitted to the frame behind the transmission. The new 80-inch twin appeared late the following year, and was designated VLDD. In 1936 the biggest twin was labeled the VLH. A competition version of the 74 was also listed in the 1935 catalog, with the designation VLDJ.

CHAPTER 2

KNUCKLEHEAD TO ELECTRA-GLIDE

The Sixty-one ohv
engine came to be known
as the Knucklehead for its
bulging rocker boxes.

Model EL 1936

In 1931 the founders had discussed plans for a new V-twin. The motor cycle would be the logical successor to the JDH, featuring more contemporary engineering, styling and performance. Meaning faster.

That summer a mock-up was built around a proposed 65-cubic inch (1065cc) flathead. The design incorporated a twin-downtube cradle frame, reinforced fork and an integrated instrument panel on the fuel tank, featuring Milwaukee's first standard-equipment speedometer. The frame and overall styling won approval, but the flathead engine was rejected. A few months later the decision was made to design and build a 61-inch (1000cc) overhead-valve engine.

Scheduled to appear as a 1935 model, progress on the 61 ohv was slowed by the effects of the Depression. Problems with oil leakage on the prototypes delayed the project further. So the debut of Milwaukee's first ohv big twin, with recirculating oil system, was postponed to 1936. Despite the delays, the new machine was an instant success.

Nicknamed the Knucklehead for its bulbous rocker boxes, the 61 ohv was

MODEL EL 1936

Engine Ohv 45° V-twin
Displacement 60.33ci (989cc)
Transmission Four-speed
Horsepower 40 @ 4800rpm
Wheelbase 59.5in (1511mm)
Weight 565lb (256kg)
Top speed 95mph (153kph)
Price $380

The first Harley-Davidson speedometer that was fitted as standard equipment.

a new motorcycle from the bottom up. The double downtube frame was necessary to handle the added power, and the early versions were not quite up to the task. The frames were strengthed for 1937. The front fork employed oval tube struts, more streamlined and stylish than the forged I-beam style used earlier. The 18-inch wheels wore 4.50-inch tires and the seat height dropped to 26 inches (66cm), lower than the Thirty-

fifty singles of a few years before.

The new engine accentuated the Sixty-one's stylishly muscular profile. The polished rocker boxes and pushrod tubes added a decorative touch to the V-twin, and drew the eye to the heart of the machine. The Knucklehead engine looked like horsepower. And the chassis' clean, unbroken line from the rear axle to the steering head was stately and strong. The consensus among most riders in 1936: the best-looking damn motorcycle they had ever seen.

And it worked. The single camshaft was more efficent and quieter than its

The Art Deco comet tank
emblem was employed from
1936 through to 1939.

two- and four-shaft flathead forebears. The hemispherical combustion chambers provided by valves set at 90 degrees meant horsepower; 37 at 4,800rpm in the standard E model, 40 from the high-compression EL. And despite the fact that a fully-fueled Knucklehead weighed in at close to 600 pounds (272kg), that was sufficient urge to propel the daring rider close to the magic 100mph (161kph).

What the Knucklehead did was look good and run strong. It had a stout dry clutch and constant-mesh four-speed transmission. The tank-mounted instrument panel and streamlined profile made it just about the most dashing looking machine on the road. Harley-Davidson had barely managed to stay afloat in the Depression years, but as the economic woes began to lift, they emerged with the right machine at the right time. And began a new chapter in the everlasting adventure, with a motorcycle tagged the Knucklehead.

A Harley-Davidson 5-gallon oil can dating from the 1930s. Collectors now pay more than $2000 for such an item in good condition.

Model VLH **1936**

The Eighty (VLH) and Seventy-four (VLD) could be ordered with the optional four-speed transmission for $15 extra. New cylinders had larger cooling fins.

The 80-inch (1340cc) flathead was introduced late in 1935 and made its official debut the following year. The big-inch twin shared with its smaller brothers new cylinder heads with larger fins and re-shaped combustion chambers. Cylinder fins were extended over the intake ports.

The Eighty shared its bore with the Seventy-four, adding displacement with a quarter-inch (6.3mm) longer stroke. The machines were otherwise identical, including the total-loss lubrication system, which would be gone the next year. Milwaukee figured the bigger twin was

MODEL VLH 1936

Engine Side-valve 45° V-twin

Displacement 80ci (1340cc)

Transmission Three- or four-speed

Horsepower 34

Wheelbase 60in (1524mm)

Weight 545lb (247kg)

Top speed 90mph (145kph)

Price $380

RIGHT: A metal authorized Harley-Davidson dealer sign, circa 1939, from the Tulsa Motorcycle Company of Oklahoma.

required for several reasons: Indian offered one, the added power would appeal to sidecarists, and the design had been proven out. Plus, it sold for $40 less than the 61 ohv, which had yet to establish its reliability.

The list of factory options had really begun growing in 1934, and a number of special equipment packages were added the next year. For 1936 the premium package included the Safety Guard (crash bars), lighted speedometer,

Jiffy Stand, Ride Control, steering damper, chrome plate group, fender lamp, stop light, dice shift knob and switch keys, saddlebags and hangers. All for $49.50.

The optional speedometers were equipped with a Maximum Speed Hand, a separate indicator that remained fixed at the highest speed attained on a ride. This was to certify one's bragging rights when comparing the motorcycle's performance with other riders' machines.

The fork spring cover was a one-year feature on the big twins, but stayed on the Forty-five for four years.

Model U **1938**

In 1937 the V series were modified and became known as the U models, with the twin downtube frame, recirculating oil system and four-speed transmission standard. The R series Forty-five was likewise revised as the W model, which also got dry-sump lubrication. Most of the improvements first seen on the 61 ohv were now incorporated throughout the Harley-Davidson lineup, and all the big twins shared a strengthened frame for 1937.

The Seventy-four now had the same stroke as the Eighty, with the bore reduced to match the 61 ohv model. This was done as a cost-saving move, so the two machines could use the same pistons. The big twin flatheads also had new cylinders with added finning, and improved bearings and oil seals in the transmission. For 1937 only, the oil tanks on all models were painted the same color as the tank and fenders. In later years the oil tank would be black.

Red and green lights replaced the ammeter and oil gauge on the instrument panel. Gone was the bronze-brown

MODEL U 1938

Engine Side-valve 45° V-twin
Displacement 73.73ci (1208cc)
Transmission Four-speed
Horsepower 34 @ 4000rpm
Wheelbase 60in (1524mm)
Weight 545lb (247kg)
Top speed 90mph (145kph)
Price $395

Military-style caps in brushed cotton were popular with motorcycle clubs in the 1930s. Club members often attached their own insignias on the front.

hue, which hadn't proven popular. Teak red with black and gold striping was still available; the new color options included venetian blue with white striping, hollywood green with gold, and silver tan with sunshine blue striping. The new striping was centered on the sides of the tank and fenders. Higher handlebars were fitted to aid handling at low speeds.

Once again the big twin frames were reinforced and given a larger backbone. The lower steering head cone was designed with a self-aligning feature to distribute force evenly on the bearings. Clutch assemblies were improved and the oil outlet fitting moved from the bottom to the rear of the oil tank.

The accessory groups became standard equipment in 1938. Customers could choose either the standard or deluxe group, which were $16.70 and $49.75 respectively. The latter added four-ply tires, Ride Control, colored shift knob, air cleaner, saddlebags and chrome trim package. The night rider could select either the pair of Little King spotlights ($11.50) or the Little Beauty pair at $13.25.

The standard Seventy-four
U model was a popular
choice for sidecars and
commercial use.

The flathead Forty-five
became the foundation of
Class C racing.

Model WLDR 1938

C lass C racing became the prominent competition category in 1938. Harley-Davidson's WLDR, rated at 27 horsepower, was the closest thing Milwaukee had to a factory racer. Since Class C was formulated as amateur racing, riders were expected to ride their machines to the track, remove unnecessary equipment, and have at it. So the WLDR was configured as a standard road model, but featured higher compression and larger valves. With the addition of aluminum heads and larger intake ports in 1939, horsepower was up into the mid-thirties.

A great measure of credit for tweaking the Forty-five's performance goes to San Jose Harley dealer Tom Sifton. As a tuner, Sifton managed to solve the breathing, lubrication and overheating difficulties magnified by racing conditions. Racer Sam Arena was soon beating the Indians, and Milwaukee incorporated most of Sifton's improvements on subsequent models. The first factory version built solely for racing, the WR, would appear in 1941.

MODEL WLDR 1938

Engine Side-valve 45° V-twin
Displacement 45.32ci (746cc)
Transmission Three-speed
Horsepower 27
Wheelbase 56.5in (1435mm)
Weight 390lb (177kg)
Top speed 85mph (137kph)
Price $380

Model EL **1939**

The Knucklehead engine was beefed up for 1939. Painted fender stripes were replaced by stainless steel strips in the same year.

The mighty Knucklehead was strengthened in 1939 with splined pinion and oil pump drive gears, and a one-piece pinion gearshaft. Stronger valve springs were also fitted, and the valve train assemblies had been completely covered the year before. All big twins in the Harley roster now had upper and lower self-aligning steering head bearings.

The instrument panel was streamlined and color matched with the motorcycle, and the design came to be called the "cat's eye" panel. The price, for the third year running, was $435.

MODEL EL 1939

Engine Ohv 45° V-twin
Displacement 60.33ci (989cc)
Transmission Four-speed
Horsepower 40 @ 4800rpm
Wheelbase 59.5in (1511mm)
Weight 565lb (256kg)
Top speed 95mph (153kph)
Price $435

Servi-Car **1941**

SERVI-CAR 1941

Engine Flathead 45° V-twin
Displacement 45.32ci
(743cc)
Transmission Three-speed
with reverse
Horsepower 22 @
4500rpm
Wheelbase 61in
(1550mm)
Weight 1,360lb (619kg)
Top speed 50mph
(80kph)
Price $510

Harley-Davidson recognized early on the commercial applications for motorcycles. Until 1930, most of Milwaukee's service vehicles employed the sidecar chassis. Rigs were modified to use open and closed sidevans, parcel cars and mail trucks.

The Servi-Car was spawned by the Cycle-Tow, which utilized an outrigger wheel on each side of the motorcyle's rear wheel. The device was sold to auto service shops as a tow vehicle to bring disabled cars in to the garage for service. It didn't work so well.

In 1932 the Servi-Car appeared as a genuine three-wheeler. The following year small or large bodies were available, and the three-speed transmission included reverse. Powered by the 45-inch (750cc) flathead, the machine was soon equipped with a towbar, bumper and spare tire mount. Final drive was by chain to a sprocket on the rear axle, which drove an automotive-type differential. The axle also carried a drum brake from the 74 VL. The Servi-Car was widely used by car dealers and repair shops, since one man could collect and

RIGHT: The flathead Forty-five proved to be the most durable motor in the Milwaukee roster. The Servi-Car was in production for more than 40 years.

return a customer's vehicle with the three-wheeler in tow. Small businesses used the trike as a delivery vehicle, but its most common application became the police transporter for emptying parking meters and writing traffic tickets.

Solo motorcylists generally scoffed at the three-wheeler, which, like the sidecar, they viewed as a bastardized union of car and motorcycle. Something to be driven, not ridden. But the practical aspects of the Servi-Car were difficult to deny. Riders who, by virtue of disability or inclination, were unable to operate a two-wheeler could still travel in the wind.

As motorcycle clubs gained increasing popularity, trike owners were welcomed as haulers of food and refreshments.

Commercial entrepreneurs on tight budgets utilized the Servi-Car as both delivery trucks and traveling billboards. The rear of the cargo box offered advertising space to display the company name and phone number.

The Servi-Car was continuously upgraded in the 1930s and 1940s, sharing many of the improvements made to the motorcycles. It gained two rear brakes in 1937 and an enclosed chain the following year. In 1939 the

towbar was strengthened and given
a permanent attachment, eliminating the
need to remove it and carry it in the trunk.
Larger bodies were offered and the rear
suspension modified.

In 1940 the axle housing was beefed
up and the transmission's shifting
mechanism was simplified. Cast iron
brake drums replaced the stamped
steel housings. A new frame was
introduced in 1941, with a stronger axle
in a welded rather than riveted tube.
The compression ratio was upped to
4.75:1 and the front brake fitted from
the Seventy-four.

Model FL **1941**

The 61 overhead-valve Knucklehead was certainly a powerful motorcycle for its day, but the American notion that bigger is better would prevail. Police forces were especially keen on top speed. The J series had established in the market an affinity for the Seventy-four, so a bigger overhead-valve twin was part of the natural progression.

The big twins had been given stronger, smoother operating clutch assemblies two years earlier. The 1939 models featured a transmission combining elements of sliding-gear and constant-mesh components, with neutral between second and third gears. The design lasted only one year. Long-distance testing on the 74 ohv prototype revealed the need for stronger crankcases, and the rocker arm assemblies were also redesigned to improve top end lubrication.

Crankpins increased in diameter, and the new crankcases for the 61 and 74 ohv lacked the baffles previously employed to equalize lubrication in the cylinders. The change helped solve

MODEL FL 1941

Engine Ohv 45° V-twin
Displacement 73.73ci (1208cc)
Transmission Four-speed
Horsepower 48 @ 5000rpm
Wheelbase 59.5in (1511mm)
Weight 575lb (261kg)
Top speed 95mph (153kph)
Price $465

RIGHT: An original Harley-Davidson one-quart oil can dating from the 1940s. The bar and shield emblem has been the most durable symbol in the Milwaukee lexicon for many decades.

the persistent problem of excessive crankcase pressure, and produced an increase in power. At the top end, larger intake ports, carburetor and redesigned manifold contributed to the horsepower gain. A new vane-type oil pump assisted in ensuring the engine's overall comfort, and a change to 5.00 x 16-inch tires provided a smoother ride. These 74-inch (1200cc) twins were designated the F and FL (higher compression) models.

Styling changed only marginally for 1941. The speedometer face changed from black numbers on white to a black background with silver numbers. The fuel tank featured a chrome band on both sides. Four color options were still available, with cruiser green replacing squadron gray on the menu. But it wasn't long before the paint selection was subordinated by the war effort, and buyers had to take what they could get.

The Knucklehead was
first offered as a
Seventy-four in 1941.

1941 was the last year
for the hot-rod Forty-five
WLDR model.

Model WLDR **1941**

Military testing had produced improvements that transferred to the civilian Forty-fives. Many big twin upgrades were applied to the little guy; the clutch assembly grew stronger and smoother in operation, and the gearbox was beefed up and given larger gears and an improved shifting mechanism.

The iron-head WL became the economy model, with compression ratio reduced to 4.75:1. The aluminum-head WLDR, on the other hand, grew even sportier with larger crankpin, stronger valve springs, hotter cams and bigger carburetor. These engines reportedly produced about 35 horsepower. It was also 1941 when the factory racing versions appeared. The WR (flat track) and WRTT (roadracing and scrambles) had flat valve lifters instead of rollers, for higher rpm.

Class C racing was achieving more popularity just as the advent of World War II put such frivolous activities on the shelf. The WLDR was discontinued during the summer, and the production of racing models was later suspended.

MODEL WLDR 1941

Engine Side-valve 45° V-twin
Displacement 45.32ci (746cc)
Transmission Three-speed
Horsepower 35 @ 5500rpm
Wheelbase 56.5in (1435mm)
Weight 390lb (177kg)
Top speed 85mph (137kph)
Price $395

The rocket-fin muffler was
quieter than its fishtail
predecessor.

Model EL 1941

The big twins received numerous improvements in the years just before the war. Aluminum heads were standard on the Eighty in 1940 and optional on the Seventy-four. The alloy cylinder head weighed over five pounds (2.27kg) less than its cast iron counterpart. Bigger crankpins, stouter clutches and constant-mesh transmissions were also incorporated the same year.

Front brake drums changed from stamped steel to stronger cast iron units; strength was added to the fork tubes by a heat treating process. The clutch lever bracket and kickstand were redesigned, and streamlined footboards replaced the previous rectangular style.

The 61 ohv E series Knucklehead now shared the heavier flywheels of the Seventy-four. The change to a half-inch (1.27cm) longer intake manifold and reduction in carburetor venturi to 1.125 inches (28.6mm) aided low-speed operation. The Sixty-one also featured the clutch upgrades applied to its bigger brethren.

MODEL EL 1941

Engine Ohv 45° V-twin
Displacement 60.33ci (989cc)
Transmission Four-speed
Horsepower 40 @ 4800rpm
Wheelbase 59.5in (1511mm)
Weight 565lb (256kg)
Top speed 95mph (153kph)
Price $425

155

Model WLA **1942**

Rumors of war were gaining momentum in 1938, and Harley-Davidson considered the prospect of preparing motorcycles for the military. The Army had been using Seventy-fours with sidecars, but was unhappy with them. Milwaukee prepared several Sixty-one ohv and Forty-five models for miltary tests.

At the time, development was underway on overhead-valve civilian versions of both the big and small flathead twins,

but the program was slowed by the military situation. In 1939 the Army conducted rigorous testing on motorcycles built by Indian, Harley-Davidson and the Delco Corporation. The latter, a BMW clone, featured shaft drive and telescopic fork. Both the Indian and Harley-Davidson were versions of each company's 750 flathead. The Army stipulated that the motorcycle must be capable of 65mph (105kph) and not overheat at low speeds.

Despite the popularity of their Chief and Scout, Indian was not in a strong

MODEL WLA 1942

Engine Side-valve 45°
V-twin
Displacement 45.12ci
(739cc)
Transmission Three-speed
Horsepower 23.5 @
4600rpm
Wheelbase 57.5in
(1460mm)
Weight 540lb (245kg)
Top speed 65mph
(105kph)
Price $380

The flathead Forty-five was the workhorse of the U.S. armed forces. Easy maintainablility was a priority.

position near the end of the decade. Their four-cylinder machine had been an expensive failure, and problems with quality control created difficulties in the marketplace. Both Indian and Harley were selling motorcycles to allied military forces overseas, and the competition for the U.S. government contracts had both companies intent on becoming the major supplier.

In March of 1940 the Army ordered 745 WLAs from Milwaukee. Harley-Davidson fitted the new style tubular front fork, which was lengthened 2.375 inches (6.03cm) to provide additional ground clearance. The olive drab machines were equipped with the new aluminum heads and D-shaped footboards, crash bars, skidplates, cargo racks and saddlebags. Orders were soon forthcoming from South Africa for 2,000 machines, 5,000 for Great Britain and another 659 for the U.S. Army. Milwaukee would later furnish military motorcycles to both the

Chinese and Russian armed forces. In its final configuration the WLA had a compression ratio of 5:1, and was rated at 23.5 horse power at 4600rpm. An oil-bath air filter was fitted, the clutch and transmission were improved, and engine lubrication was upgraded with the use of a bypass valve calibrated to engine speed. By the end of the war, Milwaukee had built some 88,000 motorcycles of this type for military use.

Model XA **1942**

By 1941 most of Harley-Davidson's production was devoted to military machines. The new 74-inch (1200cc) overhead-valve FL was introduced, but fewer than 2,500 were built. The Army had long insisted on a prototype BMW-style, shaft-drive motorcycle. Milwaukee, though hardly convinced of the necessity for such a machine, responded with the XA.

The 45 cubic inch (750cc) flathead opposed twin was a frank copy of the BMW. It featured a foot-shift four-speed transmission, shaft-drive, hand clutch, plunger rear

MODEL XA 1942

Engine Side-valve opposed twin
Displacement 45.04ci (738cc)
Transmission Four-speed
Horsepower 23 @ 4600rpm
Wheelbase 58.75in (1492mm)
Weight 538lb (244kg)
Top speed 65mph (105kph)
Price $870

Harley-Davidson
was reluctant to build the
shaft-drive XA model.

suspension and a lengthened WLA fork. The Army ordered 1,000 machines at a cost of $870 each. Production ended when the military decided that the WLA would do the job at considerably less expense. A prototype sidecar version of the boxer twin was also constructed, with a shaft driving the sidecar wheel. Development work was also underway on a shaft-drive three-wheeler, but the creation of the Jeep canceled both projects.

Model FL **1946**

The spring fork shock absorber first appeared in 1946. The rear view mirror was included in the special solo group, which included safety guards and trip odometer.

Production of the F-series Knuckle-heads jumped from fewer than 1,000 for 1945 to more than 4,000 for 1946, and rose to over 7,000 the succeeding year. The Seventy-four was outselling the Sixty-one by a significant margin.

The stylish cat's-eye instrument panel made its last appearance in 1946. The speedometer face was two-tone rather than silver, with the numerals matching the color of the inner circle. The three color combinations offered were black/silver, green/cream and gray/white in a design known as the

MODEL FL 1946

Engine Ohv 45° V-twin
Displacement 73.73ci (1208cc)
Transmission Four-speed
Horsepower 48 @ 5000rpm
Wheelbase 59.5in (1511mm)
Weight 575lb (261kg)
Top speed 95mph (153kph)
Price $465

RIGHT: The writing was on the wall for the Knucklehead by 1946. Harley-Davidson was working on the development of an improved engine that would make its debut two years later.

"airplane-style" speedometer. This would also be the last installment of the streamlined tail light, more evidence that the Art Deco influence was fading in favor of more squarish designs.

Wartime material shortages were still apparent early in the year. Gray and red were the only color options available until about mid-year, when skyway blue and black were offered once again by Harley-Davidson. Chrome tank badges and stainless steel trim were also absent from the earlier models, and likewise for chromed shift levers and gates, headlight rims and gas caps.

Few more than 2,000 ohv models had been produced in Milwaukee during the war, and most were for military use. But testing and development continued during this period, as Harley-Davidson looked ahead to the prospects in the post-war market. Work on the first hydraulic telescope front fork was underway, and a prototype was fitted to a Knucklehead in 1945. The Hydra-Glide fork would appear on production models in 1949.

The first indication of hydraulic damping for the front wheel appeared on the big twins in 1946. A Monroe

Seat options were limited
in availablity just after
the war. The deluxe solo
saddle still rode atop the
Ful-Floteing spring.

shock absorber adjoined the fork springs, replacing the rudimentary Ride-Control friction device.

No corresponding cushioning occured at the rear wheel, which remained solidly bolted to the frame. Suspension advancements in Milwaukee would evidently be addressed strictly one end at a time.

The Knucklehead itself was now on the road to history. Notwithstanding its reputation for caution in developing new models, Milwaukee recognized that motorcycling would soon be changing. That more riders would be demanding

LEFT: The airplane-style speedometer was fitted from 1941 through 1946. The two-tone face was either black/silver, green/cream or gray/white.

smoother, oil-tight engines, motors that started easily and were reliable (even for the mechanically disinclined), and transmissions that shifted without the removal of a hand from the handlebar.

Model FL 1947

The biggest change in Harley-Davidson's 1947 models was the price. The cost of the top-of-the-line 74 overhead valve had held steady at $465 for six years, although very few were produced from 1941-45. The price in 1947 on the last of the Seventy-four Knuckleheads was $605, a 33 percent jump from the year before. Inflation was soaring, and indulging in peacetime recreation was evidently going to be expensive.

A number of revisions were made for 1947 that distinguish the final Knucklehead from its predecessors. Streamlining was back in the form of new fuel tank nameplates, which came to be called "speed ball" badges. Stainless steel fender trim returned to production, as did the front fender lamp. A larger tail light, nicknamed the "tombstone" design, incorporated the license plate bracket.

The fuel tank was redesigned to accommodate a new instrument panel, and the speedometer face featured a

MODEL FL 1947

Engine Ohv 45° V-twin
Displacement 73.73ci (1208cc)
Transmission Four-speed
Horsepower 48 @ 5000rpm
Wheelbase 59.5in (1511mm)
Weight 575lb (261kg)
Top speed 95mph (153kph)
Price $605

RIGHT: This Harley-Davidson dealer clock with bar and shield emblem dates from 1947, the last year of Knucklehead production.

two-tone black and white background on which were italicized silver numerals and a red pointer. The separate generator and oil lights were consolidated in a small rectangular housing with a single lens situated in the center of the tank.

The Deluxe Buddy Seat had been deleted during the war years and returned to civilian duty in 1946. The 1947 version was offered in black cowhide only, featuring a plastic skirt with a chromed star attached on each side.

Four color options were again offered in 1947: skyway blue, cruiser green, flight red and brilliant black. Nearly 12,000 Knuckleheads were made for the model year, over half Milwaukee's total production. In its twelve-year run the Knuckle had won a loyal following, and remains an icon in the Harley lineage as the original American superbike.

The tombstone taillight first appeared in 1947. Chrome exhaust pipe covers and fender tips came with the special solo group.

125 Model S **1948**

Harley-Davidson was the only U.S. motorcycle manufacturer in a strong position before, during and after the war. Among the most tangible spoils of victory was the appropriation of Germany's DKW manufacturing rights, which Milwaukee shared with BSA of Great Britain. Thus the instant lightweight. Small two-stroke motorcycles had never achieved wide popularity in the United States, and the S model would prove no exception. But it did provide benefits for Harley-Davidson in the long term. The tiddler offered a low-cost entry into motorcycling ($5.50 per week), and surely stimulated the appetites of young novice riders for bigger and better machines. Preferably, from the Milwaukee viewpoint, bigger and better motorcycles with valves.

DKW (Dampf Kraft Wagen) had built some fast racing motorcycles, but the proletarian 125 was simply an economical utility machine. They served well as mass transportation on the congested byways of Europe, but

125 MODEL S 1948

Engine Two-stroke single
Displacement 7.6ci (125cc)
Transmission Three-speed
Horsepower 3
Wheelbase 50in (1270mm)
Weight 185lb (84kg)
Top speed 50mph (80kph)
Price $325

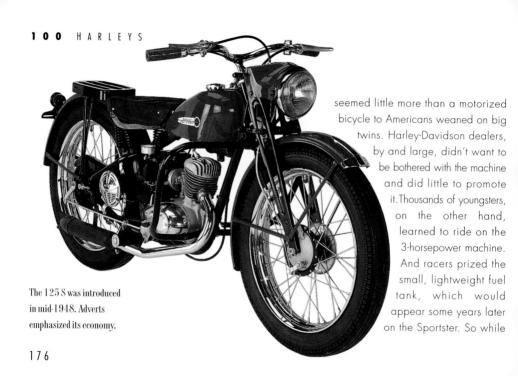

The 125 S was introduced
in mid-1948. Adverts
emphasized its economy.

seemed little more than a motorized
bicycle to Americans weaned on big
twins. Harley-Davidson dealers,
by and large, didn't want to
be bothered with the machine
and did little to promote
it. Thousands of youngsters,
on the other hand,
learned to ride on the
3-horsepower machine.
And racers prized the
small, lightweight fuel
tank, which would
appear some years later
on the Sportster. So while

the S model never became a sales leader, it did evolve into a multi-purpose machine later tagged the Hummer, and expand in displacement to 165 and 175cc off-road variants.

The S model turned out to be a good (and inexpensive) investment in Harley-Davidson's future. It enticed a good number of young folks into the exhilarating sport of motorcycling. And, with almost perfect timing, it taught them how to clutch with the hand and shift with the foot. That process would soon accelerate with the arrival of other more substantial motorcycles from overseas.

Model FL **1948**

NEW! IMPROVED! No other two words figured more strongly in American advertising after World War II. As applied to motorcycle engines they usually meant overhead valves, hydraulic lifters, aluminum heads, improved lubrication and better combustion. Enter the Panhead. Not that the new FL was an entirely new engine, as the Knucklehead had been 12 years before. Harley-Davidson product development has always been evolutionary. The frame was stretched to accommodate the taller engine, which was lighter and carried its oil lines inside. A new oil pump did a more thorough job of sending lubricant to the required parts. But the most distinctive departure from the past was the Panhead's hydraulic valve lifters, which solved two problems. Maintaining exact valve adjustment became less critical and the engine ran cooler.

With the Panhead, Milwaukee set out to make motorcycling easier. Heretofore the sport was largely limited to those capable of maintaining, and often repairing, an unforgiving mechanical

MODEL FL 1948

Engine Ohv 45° V-twin
Displacement 73.73ci (1208cc)
Transmission Four-speed
Horsepower 50 @ 4800rpm
Wheelbase 59.5in (1511mm)
Weight 565lb (256kg)
Top speed 100mph (161kph)
Price $650

RIGHT: Aluminum heads, hydraulic lifters and cake pan valve covers distinguished the Panhead from the Knucklehead. In most other respects, the engines were identical. The springer front end would be gone the following year.

assemblage. Motorcycles that ran better and longer without expert attention were likely to attract new riders.

The engine's bottom end was largely unchanged. A new camshaft was designed for the new valve system, and the cases modified for the new cylinders. The frame was tagged the "wishbone" for its bowed downtubes, and incorporated a steering head lock and mounting plate for crash bars. With the advent of the Hydra-Glide front fork in 1949, the '48 grew to become a prized model – the first Panhead and the last Springer. Like the Knuckle, the Pan's

designations were E for the Sixty-one and F for the Seventy-four.

Horsepower was only marginally higher for the new engine, but it was generally more reliable power. The pan-shaped valve covers kept more oil inside the motor, and the aluminum heads reduced operating temperatures on long rides and in hot weather. The new system was not trouble-free, of course. From 1948 through 1952 the hydraulic lifters rode atop the pushrods, and a low oil supply could cause malfunction. In 1953 the lifters were relocated to housings above the timing case.

E & FL Hydra-Glide **1951**

MODEL FL 1951

Engine Ohv 45° V-twin
Displacement 73.73ci
(1208cc)
Transmission Four-speed
Horsepower 55 @
4800rpm
Wheelbase 59.5in
(1511mm)
Weight 590lb (268kg)
Top speed 100mph
(161kph)
Price $900

Harley-Davidson leaped into the present in 1949 with the introduction of the Hydra-Glide front fork. Not long after the war, Milwaukee realized that more British and European motorcycles were headed for the U.S.A. And that the imported machines had hydraulic suspension systems. And that these motorcycles were fast.

How the foreign makes would be received by American riders remained uncertain in 1950. But Harley-Davidson was not so hidebound by tradition that they could wait and see. Even though Indian was in serious decline, that meant only that new competitors would arise. So the process of evolutionary development and refinement of the big twins continued, albeit with the measured pragmatism for which Milwaukee was known. The Hydra-Glide fork served two functions. With two hydraulic/spring tubes, more compliant suspension brought a smoother ride. Secondly, it looked more contemporary. For both cars and motorcycles, the trend in the 1950s was to cover up more of the

The 1951 FL
Hydra-Glide. The solo
windshield was a
$21.00 optional extra.

Optional bumpers, available for both front and rear fenders, were known as "cheese graters."

mechanical bits. Designers moved to more rounded, seamless shapes that reflected the New Modern Age.

The styling shift was also apparent in the fenders, more deeply skirted, one-piece units with contours unbroken by seams or stripes. Parking lamps adorned the upper fork cover and the horn was moved down between the frame tubes. The fuel tanks still carried the subdued nameplate, created by automotive designer Brooks Stevens, that first appeared in 1947. In 1951 the name-plates changed to a script-style logo on a bar background.

It was during this period that Milwaukee discovered what's in a name. Harley-Davidson motorcycles had always been designated only with model letters preceded by a number indicating engine displacement, as in 61 EL. The bikes' nicknames – Silent Gray Fellow, Panhead, Peashooter, Knucklehead – were monikers conferred after the fact by riders themselves. Even the Hydra-Glide was not actually a model name, but rather a label for the new front fork. In 1952 The Motor Company (a contraction by early employees) used Hydra-Glide as a distinct model name on the order blanks. Three years later the two-stroke S model became the Hummer, and in 1957 the new XL would be christened with one of motorcycling's most winning appellations, the Sportster. And a year later, when the first big twin with shock absorbers at both ends rolled off the line, its title was prominently displayed on the front fender: Duo-Glide. Since then, but for racing models,

LEFT: This is the smaller Sixty-one EL Panhead, a 1950 model. The celebrated Hydra-Glide front fork offered a smoother ride and a more contemporary look.

The Speed King leather
saddlebag was first
offered as an accessory
in 1954.

no Harley-Davidson has gone nameless down the road.

Rewind to 1950: concurrent with the drift to less ornate motorcycles came increasing options in accessories. Milwaukee had noted the pride most riders took in outfitting the machines according to their individual tastes. The term Full Dress entered the lexicon, later distilled to Dresser, meaning a motorcycle bedecked in full touring regalia. Harley-Davidson expanded both its line of add-on hardware and the selection of functional yet fashionable motorcyling apparel.

The Panhead was effectively Milwaukee's first easy rider. A big motorcycle, topping 600 pounds (272kg) on the scales fully dressed, built for comfort not for speed. Yes, it could be pushed to around 100mph (161kph) and the rubber-mounted handlebar ignored some of the vibration, but the engine was not happy. The adult portion of the 55 horsepower lived between 3500 and 4500rpm, plenty enough to motor smartly along. A larger front brake offered a bit more assistance in getting the big twin slowed down.

BELOW: Harley-Davidson remains acutely aware of its heritage. This contemporary wristwatch is sold in an embossed tin Panhead case.

189

A 1951 FL. The Panhead
engine was rated at 55
horsepower.

FL & FLF Hydra-Glide 1952

S ome of the veteran Harley-Davidson fraternity, now accompanied by a growing sorority, were stunned with the 1952 option of foot-shift (the designation for this version being FLF). Many riders never considered the foot clutch/hand-shift system a major inconvenience. That's how cars operated, so what the hell. But most, after riding one and swapping the functions of hand and foot, noted the new ease of riding in traffic. In retrospect, the old method seemed like monkey motion.

Hand-shift was still available on both the Sixty-one and Seventy-four, and would remain in the catalog until 1972 when there were too few geezers left to matter. For the second year running, only the high-compression models were offered for both the Sixty-one and Seventy-four now officially called Hydra-Glides. Since the hand-lever was fitted to the left handlebar, the brake lever moved to the other side and aligned Milwaukee with the rest of the world. Except Great Britain, whose motorcycles had right-side shift levers and left-side brake levers.

MODEL FLF 1952

Engine Ohv 45° V-twin
Displacement 73.73ci (1208cc)
Transmission Four-speed
Horsepower 55 @ 4800rpm
Wheelbase 59.5in (1511mm)
Weight 590lb (268kg)
Top speed 100mph (161kph)
Price $970

In 1951 the sidecar added $240 to the cost of the Hydra-Glide.

This was the final year for the 61-inch (1000cc) Panhead. The Seventy-four outsold the smaller twin by a greater margin each year, and Milwaukee saw no reason to offer two such similar machines. Given the stout nature of the clutch springs, the hand-clutch model was fitted with a leverage booster which came to be called a "mouse trap."

The Panhead was not entirely free of the top-end oiling problems that had nagged the Knucklehead. Difficulties with dirty oil clogging the lifters was addressed with a check valve and filter screen. This worked until the screen itself clogged up. and choked the oil supply. The problem was eliminated in 1953 when the lifters moved from the tops to the bottoms of the pushrods.

Another top end modification for 1952 was the rotating exhaust valve. In an effort to prevent burned valves, a cap between the valve stem and rocker allowed the valve to rotate when open. This worked to equalize the wear pattern and maintain good compression.

A 1952 FLF. The first foot-shift Panhead had a clutch booster system called the "mouse trap."

Model K 1952

Brand new in '52: the Sports Model Forty-five twin didn't ignite many bonfires of popularity. But it had swingarm rear suspension, hand clutch and foot-shift. Good signs.

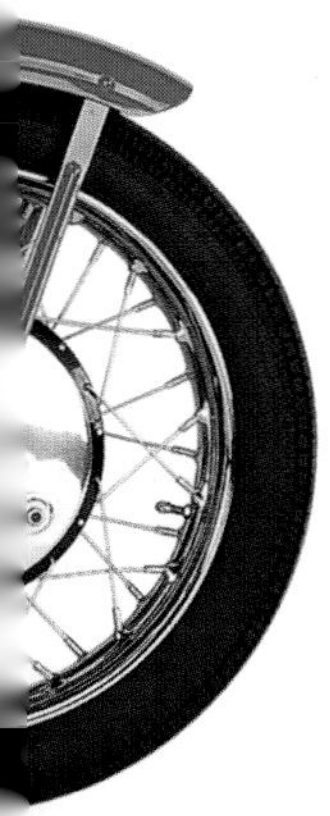

1952 saw a new model in a distinguished and long-lived family of motorcycles take the stage; it was still a 45-inch (750cc) flathead, but otherwise a workhorse of an entirely different order. As the first D model of 1929 had begat the R of '32, which sired the W in 1937, the K model became the sole surviving son in the flathead family tree.

While the engine was entirely new, improved was another matter. The K engine was a thoroughly contemporary design, incorporating the transmission in the crankcases, foot-shifter on the right side and a hand clutch. And, compared

MODEL K 1952

Engine Side-valve 45° V-twin
Displacement 45.32ci (743cc)
Transmission Four-speed
Horsepower 30
Wheelbase 56.5in (1435mm)
Weight 400lb (181kg)
Top speed 80mph (129kph)
Price $865

to the Panhead, it looked downright sporty. But the style went unreflected by the machine's performance, which was widely described as moderate to mediocre. Some said it was just slow.

With hydraulic suspension at both ends, the K handled better than its springer antecedents.

On the other hand, the K was the first Harley-Davidson with forks in the plural. One at the front and one at the rear, commonly called a swingarm. With hydraulic suspension at both ends, the motorcycle demonstrated better handling than its springer/rigid predecessor, but with 30 horsepower hauling 400 pounds (181kg) the envelope was lightly pushed. To Milwaukee's added misfortune, the K bike arrived just as the Korean War was heating up and overall motorcycle sales were in decline.

On yet another hand, the new flathead served well in racing trim. Since

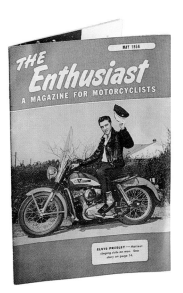

The May 1956 issue of Harley-Davidson's house journal *The Enthusiast* featured the young Elvis Presley on a Model K on the cover. Now it's a valuable collectible in its own right.

racing had resumed after the war, Harley-Davidson hadn't won at Daytona Beach. Six times in a row the competition had prevailed, and for the last four years running the victor (three times Dick Klamfoth, once Billy Mathews) had ridden a British Norton. This caused some moodiness in Milwaukee, which had won three of the five pre-war events. Corrective measures would be taken.

Out on the American highways it was another matter. Young hot-rodders hoping for a hopped-up Harley were getting smoked by overhead-valve 500cc Triumph and BSA twins. Milwaukee recognized the need for a sporting ohv motorcycle, and in fact had one in development, but cautionary advance was still the rule. Racing had shown that more power could be had from the flathead, and the simple route was an increase in displacement. Development work on a single-cam, overhead-valve engine designated the KL, was shelved. Work would proceed on an ohv engine called the XL, based on the K model's four-cam configuration.

So the K model, as a 750, lasted only two years. Total production on the K model for two years was 3,693.

LEFT: The K model had its gears inside the crankcase, the term for which is unit construction. Four single-lobed cams opened and closed the valves.

The new tank emblem
in 1955 incorporated a
large V motif.

FLH Hydra-Glide **1955**

Milwaukee had jacked up the performance curve on the K model in 1954, and decided that the FL was also eligible for more muscle. The first of several new components was an improved intake manifold, employing O-rings to improve sealing and accommodate a measure of vibration. Intake tracts were cast into the new heads, eliminating the threaded nipples used before. The new hot-rod heavyweight appeared in mid-1955 and was naturally designated the

FLH. Compression ratio was up to 8.0:1 and the H was rated at 60 horsepower. The bottom end was given stoutness in the form of stronger cases and bigger bearings.

The FL series also premiered a number of styling changes in 1955. The V-twin configuration was extended to the tank emblem, which incorporated a large V behind the Harley-Davidson script logo. The new fork top panel was decorated with three diagonal stripes on each side, and the Hydra-Glide insignia was discontinued. The tombstone tail light was replaced by an oval unit.

MODEL FLH 1955

Engine Ohv 45° V-twin
Displacement 73.73ci (1208cc)
Transmission Four-speed
Horsepower 60 @ 4800rpm
Wheelbase 59.5in (1511mm)
Weight 598lb (271kg)
Top speed 105mph (169kph)
Price $1,083

The KH was a stroked K
model. Displacement
increased to 883cc.

Models KH & KHK **1955-56**

Following its customary letter designations, Milwaukee added an H to the K model in 1954. Fans seeking to apply some retrospective rationale to the Harley-Davidson lettering system have offered Hot, Heavy Duty and High Compression as possibilities. Hmm.

As an added letter, the H first appeared in 1915 as identification of a Fast Motor, Roadster Racer and a Track Racer. Then the letter disappeared from the roster until 1929, when the JD got an H

to designate the twin-cam engine. So the mysterious H may simply be the traditional letter for the High performance version of an existing engine. Or Hero, or Hell-on-wheels.

In 1954 the H meant an additional three-quarter inch (19mm) of stroke, which upped the displacement to 54 cubic inches (883cc). This translated into a jumbo increase in torque and a tendency for the transmission gears to shred teeth. The gears were made stronger, and with its larger valves the KH cranked out a claimed 38 horsepower. Top speed was up to

MODEL KH 1955

Engine Side-valve 45° V-twin
Displacement 54ci (883cc)
Transmission Four-speed
Horsepower 38
Wheelbase 56.5in (1435mm)
Weight 400lb (181kg)
Top speed 95mph (153kph)
Price $925

In 1955 the KH speedometer was rubber-mounted. The motorcycle was good for 95mph (153kph).

95mph (153kph), and according to a *Cycle Magazine* test, the new model was two seconds quicker in the quarter-mile. The elapsed time was 14.75 seconds.

Next came the model KHK in 1955. (Alphabet historians will note that the K also first appeared in 1915, to designate a "stripped stock" racing model.) The extra K meant that for $68 a Speed Kit was installed at the factory, which included a roller-bearing

bottom end, hot rod cams and polished ports. Unlike the earlier models, the transmission in the 1954-'56 K models could be accessed without splitting the cases. The bike weighed about 440 pounds (200kg).

In 1956 the KH was fitted with slightly shorter shock absorbers, although wheel travel remained the same. The oil pump was strengthened and the rear wheel got roller bearings in place of the former double-row ball bearings. The big twin tail light replaced the old bullet-style lamp, and a bold stroke of color appeared on the fuel tank. The model

ABOVE: Commemorative
50th Anniversary badge.
LEFT: A 1956 KHK. This
variant was the hot-rod
of the family.

Externally the KH and
KHK were identical but for
the oil tank decal.

shown here features the new color, champion yellow. Flamboyant metallic green was available at extra cost. The K and KH models occupy a curious niche in Harley-Davidson history, given their brief production runs. In its four-year span the total KH output was 2,824. Total production for the KHK was 1,163. The factory records are sketchy on the KR racing versions, but perhaps fewer than 500 were built over 15 years.

XL Sportser **1957**

Few people were expecting the Sportster. Insiders knew that another overhead-valve twin was in the works, and that the new cylinders would be bolted to the K model bottom end. Hopes were not exceptionally high.

But the doubters were all but dumbstruck when the XL showed up lean and mean and ready for the green. Hot rodding had become a booming national sport in 1955. When the signal came from Detroit, in the form of the square-shouldered Chevrolet coupé with a 265ci (4.3lit)

V-8, the flags went up. Horsepower in the streets. By 1957 "three-quarter race" engines were rumbling at stoplights all over this land. And ka-thumping right there alongside them were Harley-Davidson Sportsters.

The Sportster perpetuated its flathead forebears' tradition of a camshaft for each valve. In addition to allowing shorter and stronger camshafts, the 4-cam design provides the pushrods more direct paths to the rocker arms and simplifies adjustments to cam timing. In stock trim the XL motor made 40 horsepower at 5500rpm, and the

MODEL XL 1957

Engine Ohv 45° V-twin
Displacement 53.9ci (883cc)
Transmission Four-speed
Horsepower 40 @ 5500rpm
Wheelbase 57in (1448mm)
Weight 495lb (225kg)
Top speed 95mph (153kph)
Price $1,103

An ohv version of the K model, designated the KL, ws built in 1952. But Milwaukee decided on the KH flathead instead. The KL became the basis of the Sportster.

compression ratio increased to 9:1. Exhaust valves were hardened with stellite facing, and the valves were much bigger than the flathead's. The engine retained the same stroke as the K model (3.81in, 97mm), but the cylinder bore grew to 3.0in (76mm). In comparative terms, the Sportster held a shorter-stroke engine that revved more quickly.

Some riders were surprised, given the Sportster's high-performance profile, that it appeared with cast iron rather than aluminum heads. Even though aluminum's superior heat dissipation was a proven factor, Milwaukee's experience

with the early Panhead had been troublesome. Rather than risk similar problems with the Sportster, which had to confront the British twins from the get-go, Harley-Davidson went with the known quantity of cast iron.

The first Sportster was obviously not an all-out roadburner. With its buckhorn bars and complement of accessories, the XL was designed as the middleweight sport-touring mount in the lineup. Only slightly more powerful, and barely faster than the KH, the 495-pound (225kg) machine reflected more of the style of high performance than the substance.

The large fuel tank and full rear fender made the motorcycle look more like a shrunken Panhead than a serious backroad blaster.

Even though the new model didn't stun the motorcycling world with its initial appearance or performance, the Sportster was obviously Milwaukee's boldest move in a long time. And although some compromises had been made to keep production costs in line, the XL made it apparent that Harley-Davidson wasn't about to forfeit a growing portion of the market to the British and European competition.

FLH Duo-Glide **1958**

MODEL FLH 1958

Engine Ohv 45° V-twin
Displacement 73.73ci
(1208cc)
Transmission Four-speed
Horsepower 52
Wheelbase 60in
(1520mm)
Weight 648lb (294kg)
Top speed 100mph
(161kph)
Price $1,320

In 1958 the Hydra-Glide was re-christened the Duo-Glide, designating the arrival of suspension components at the rear wheel. The rigid frame was replaced with a swing arm and hydraulic shock absorbers, and both the FL and FLH were still offered with either hand- or foot-shift.

By now the foot-shifter was outselling the hand-shift model by three to one. A new marriage of convenience and necessity had been conducted in Milwaukee. Harley-Davidson was selling some 12,000 motorcycles annually for seven years running. The demise of Indian had effected the widening ripple of British dealerships in the U.S.A. The game was on again.

Competition works implicitly to improve the product, not only in racing but at the engineer's drawing table and the designer's sketch pad. The impulse to solve the problem, whether higher performance, comfort, durability or style, the driving force is making it work properly. And better than the other fellow's. The Duo-Glide had not only new shocks, but a hydraulic rear

brake, new oil tank, tougher transmission and clutch, tighter exhaust manifold connectors, and optional white wall tires. Cylinder head fins were larger, the FLH got stronger valve springs, and dual exhausts with short mufflers were also available as an option. Without the rigid frame as fender mount, chromed struts extended aft of the upper shock mounts to support the mudguard, which was still hinged for tire-changing chores. The new front crash bar was a one-piece unit.

New bumpers for the front and rear fenders were introduced in '58. The tank nameplates were plastic, replaced a

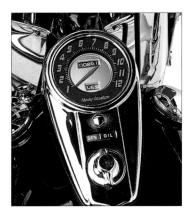

RIGHT: The Duo-Glide emblem on the fender
distinguishes the '58 from earlier models.

year later by metal. The color options included skyline blue/white, calypso red/white, sabre gray metallic/white and black/white.

In 1959 the circular nameplate was replaced by an oval background for a chrome arrow with Harley-Davidson inscribed. Like the previous badge, the new design was used for only two years. The foot-shift model had a neutral indicator light on the instrument panel. New metal front and rear fender tips replaced the plastic versions, and the toolbox featured an optional chrome cover.

This is a 1959 FLH;
note the new style of
tank nameplate.
This design only lasted
for two years.

XLCH Sportster **1958**

Entering its second year of production, the Sportster got two burly brothers. The XL remained the standard-issue model, while the XLH featured higher compression and the XLCH was offered as a competition scrambler. Horsepower was up in 1958, with bigger ports and valves, stronger gears and better oil sealing. The CH was created in response to pressure from California racers, who wanted to challenge the more nimble British twins. The original edition had twin straight exhaust pipes, painted not chromed, a bobbed rear fender, no lights and wide-ratio gearing. The fuel tank, which would come to be known as the peanut tank, was pirated from the 125cc Hummer.

The Sportster was thus destined to have two distinct identities, and generate several more hybrid versions, during the next 15 years. The XL and XLH versions were developed in Milwaukee's traditional fashion of incremental improvements from year to year. As

MODEL XLCH 1958

Engine Ohv 45° V-twin
Displacement 53.9ci (883cc)
Transmission Four-speed
Horsepower 45
Wheelbase 57in (1448mm)
Weight 480lb (218kg)
Top speed 115mph (185kph)
Price $1,155

RIGHT: The original XLCH was set up as an off-road machine, but could easily be modified for the street. Even in road trim, it is a powerfully aggressive-looking motorcycle.

sporting middleweights in the American idiom, the road model Sportsters were logical derivatives of the KH model. The XLH was more powerful, and became a reasonable option for riders who didn't care for the bulk and weight of the FL.

The XLCH, on the other hand, became the production prototype for all manner of snorting tire-smokers for the road and track. First, it was available with a 19-inch front wheel which meant more ground clearance and stability in off-road conditions. Without the baggage of battery, lights, mufflers and chrome appointments, it weighed about 40

Straight pipes are the original configuration, but have been lengthened for top end performance.

pounds (18kg) less than the road model. And with the proper application of throttle and clutch, the XLCH emitted an enormous roar followed by a cloud of rubber-burning smoke, until it caught traction and shot down the road in some haste.

The XLCH was an instant hit with many riders who had no off-road ambitions. So in 1959 the sportier Sportster arrived in legal highway trim: muffler, lights, bigger fenders and chromium-plated accessories. Which was exactly what the hot-rod riders wanted, a street/dirt bike.

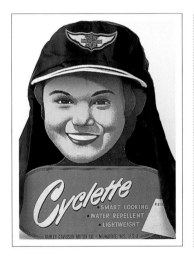

LEFT: The Cyclette cap was aimed at women riders of the 1950s. The foreign legion-style apron helped protect ladies' hair from the effects of wind, rain and grime.

The first Sprints imported
bore the Italian logo
on the tank.

Sprint **1961**

In 1960 Harley-Davidson bought half-interest in the Italian firm of Aeronautica Macchi, which built single-cylinder, two- and four-stroke machines. Milwaukee knew the lightweight market was on the way up, and that the Hummer-derived two-strokes would not be competitive. The 250cc Sprint was intoduced in 1961. The ohv single hung horizontally in a single-strut frame, which made it distinctive on American roads. The base engine had compression of 8.5:1 and produced 18 horsepower at 6750 rpm. The styling was not an instant hit with U.S. riders.

But the Sprint had a capable engine for its displacement, and had already shown its gumption in European road-racing. Once again Americans were keen to find out what it would do in the dirt, so the Sprint soon evolved into dual-purpose trail-bike/racer formats. The initial C model was joined in 1962 by the H rendition, a street-scrambler with smaller tank, seat, high front fender and exhaust pipe. The Sprint H later became the Scrambler and then the Sprint SS. The racing model was designated CRS.

SPRINT 1961

Engine Ohv horizontal single
Displacement 15ci (246cc)
Transmission Four-speed
Horsepower 18 @ 6750rpm
Wheelbase 52in (1320mm)
Weight 275lb (125kg)
Top speed 75mph (121kph)
Price $690

XLR Sportster **1962**

The Sportster continued its evolution with the XLR, which was built for TT scrambles racing. At a glance the R appeared to be simply an XLCH stripped for competition, but the engine had a number of differences. The only obvious hint was the magneto mounted ahead of the front cylinder, rather than on the right hand side. The XLR ran ball bearings at the crankshaft ends and different heads, flywheels, cams, pistons and valves. In the hands of factory riders Mert Lawwill and Mark Brelsford, the machines were wicked fast on the track. With the aid of tuner Jim Belland, the motors were good for about 80 horsepower and the bike weighed little over 350 pounds (159kg). Brelsford, whose motorcycle was nicknamed Goliath, was one of the few riders to explore its limits.

The XLR engine was produced in limited numbers, probably fewer than 500 in a ten-year period. But until the rules changed and it was supplanted

MODEL XLR 1962

Engine Ohv 45° V-twin
Displacement 53.9ci (883cc)
Transmission Four-speed
Horsepower 80
Wheelbase 57in (1448mm)
Weight 350lb (159kg)
Top speed 115mph (185kph)
Price $1,245

The XLR, overhead-valve successor to the KR, was built for the sole purpose of winning races. It was offered with a wide variety of sprockets to afford racers a range of gearing choices for different tracks.

by the XR 750, the XLR was the horsepower king. The engine was used in many drag racing machines, and powered the Manning/Riley/Rivera streamliner that Cal Rayborn aimed to a new record of 265.49mph (426.5kph) at Bonneville Salt Flats in Utah in October 1970.

Note: William G. Davidson joined the company in 1963 as director of styling. As the son of former president William H. and grandson of founder William A. Davidson, Willie G. had some sense of the family business. He has held the position for 36 years.

The XLR looked even
meaner and nastier than
the civilian XLCH.

The XLCH established the
Sportster Look that was to
prevail to the present day.

XLCH & XLH 1964

Stylistic changes were few in 1964. The XLH Sportster received a full-width front brake hub fashioned of aluminum by the Aermacchi branch, and the company logo was redesigned to fit the fashion of the times. A center stand, officially named the Jiffy Stand, was now standard equipment on both models. In 1965 the Sportster was granted a 12-volt electrical system, and the gas tank was slightly smaller. Spark advance on the XLH became automatic, while the XLCH retained its manual advance that was located on the left handgrip.

The XLCH lean machine saw only minor modifications until 1966 when a new carburetor and high-performance cams bumped the horsepower to about 60. This year also marked the advent of the "ham can" air cleaner cover, the result of federal emissions controls.

The larger Tillotson carburetor featured a diaphragm and accelerator pump. The new cams, designated the P profile, bumped the power in the middle and upper segments of the rev range. The CH was a certified road warrior, but for

MODEL XLCH 1964

Engine Ohv 45° V-twin
Displacement 53.9ci (883cc)
Transmission Four-speed
Horsepower 45
Wheelbase 57in (1448mm)
Weight 480lb (218kg)
Top speed 110mph (177kph)
Price $1,360

A dealer postcard urging customers to "drop in and see the 1964 models." The couple are riding an FL Duo-Glide. The Sportsters were marginally cheaper.

the novice it could be a bitch to kickstart. Knowing the precise priming drill helped but didn't always light the engine before the operator was slumped sweating at the curb.

The problem was solved on the XLH in 1967 when an electric starter was fitted. The hard-core macho boys took this as heresy, and derided the "electric leg" crowd as sissies. But so long as the battery was charged, the sissies didn't much care. The 12-volt battery and oil tank fitted to a rubber-mounted platform, and the smaller headlight resided in a compact nacelle.

The XLCH shared the new cases, with provision for the electric starter, but remained a kicker. In 1969 the magneto was replaced by an ignition timer/coil system which made starting easier. Two years later the ignition moved inside the timing case where it was better protected from the elements.

Approaching the 1970s, the H and CH Sportsters were losing their individual identities. Development of the racing version had shifted to the XR 750, a short-stroke version of the XLR. Milwaukee set about upgrading the Sportster in traditional fashion – more cubic inches.

Sportster options
included windshield,
spotlights and Buddy
Seat in white or
black & white.

FLH Electra-Glide **1965**

The Duo- becomes Electra-, and the perennial Panhead makes its final appearance. With the addition of an electric starter, and the name Electra-Glide, the 74-inch (1200cc) Panhead meets its 18th and final year of production. Retired after mostly meritorious service.The mantle of first thumb start/last Panhead has ensured collector status for the '65 Electra-Glide, combining as it does an end and a beginning. The first electric-start big twin carries the freight of Historical Significance.

And properly so. Milwaukee was witnessing the greatest leap in motorcycle sales in U.S. history, and was determined to be more than just a spectator. Harley-Davidson's sales figures had been more or less static for ten years, and Panheads accounted for roughly half the total each year. But with the stunning ascent of Honda, soaring motorcycle sales made the old graph obsolete. And for 1965, H-D built more Panheads (6,930) than any year since its debut in 1948.

MODEL FLH 1965

Engine Ohv 45° V-twin
Displacement 73.73ci (1208cc)
Transmission Four-speed
Horsepower 60 @5400rpm
Wheelbase 60in (1524mm)
Weight 783lb (355kg)
Top speed 100mph (161kph)
Price $1,595

RIGHT: This speedometer, nicknamed the "tombstone," was used from 1962-67.

FAR RIGHT: The rocket-fin look returned with the Super-Quiet muffler, used on the big twins from 1962-66. Fiberglass saddlebags first appeared in 1963.

So '65 was a seminal year that came to represent Milwaukee's transition to the Modern Age of American motorcycling. With 12-volt electrics came a new frame to accommodate the large battery, the new oil tank moved to the left side and the foot-shift model got a 5-gallon (18.9lit) fuel tank. A new cast aluminum primary cover was fashioned to support the electric leg.

Once again the motive was to make

motorcycling easier, since it was now established that the market for user-friendly machines was larger than anyone had previously imagined. Spark advance was now handled automatically, eliminating the cable-operated mechanism. And although the Electra-Glide's engine internals were unchanged, stronger cases and clutch were also dictated by the starter. The new primary covers held the transmission in fixed position, so primary chain adjustment was done through an access hole in the cover.

The Electra-Glide differed from prior Pans in several other ways. The domed caps were gone from the shock absorbers, since the upper shock mount also served to attach the rear crash bar. The trumpet horn was replaced by a disc unit fitted below the headlight, and the ribbed timing cover was supplanted by a smooth aluminum casting. Ball-end aluminum clutch and brake levers made their first appearance, and the toolbox was eliminated by the large 12-volt battery.

CHAPTER 3

CHANGING FORTUNES

FLH Electra-Glide **1966**

Milwaukee wasn't entirely prepared for the motorcycle sales boom of the mid-1960s. In some quarters that might qualify as an understatement, but few prophets predicted the social or economic upheavals of the times that were "a changin". Harley-Davidson, as ever, charted its own course.

As the Electra-Glide had grown in size and weight, the demands on the engine increased in proportion. Economic realities would not permit a completely new engine, so Milwaukee settled for a new top end. And although conceived in terms of functional improvement, the Shovelhead (as it came to be known) displayed a return to the forms of yesteryear. With its rocker boxes in lieu of covers, the Shovel recalled the stying cues of the mighty Knucklehead of the 1930s.

The new cylinder head was a larger aluminum version of the Sportster lid, with the same combustion chamber and valve angle. The more efficient respiration was good for an increase of five horsepower. With the power gain came a corresponding rise in vibration, but most fans of the full dressers counted

MODEL FLH 1966

Engine Ohv 45° V-twin
Displacement 73.73ci (1208cc)
Transmission Four-speed
Horsepower 54 @ 5400rpm
Wheelbase 60in (1524mm)
Weight 783lb (355kg)
Top speed 100mph (161kph)
Price $1,610

RIGHT: In 1966 the Panhead's valve covers gave way to rocker boxes, which led to the engine's Shovelhead nickname. The "ham can" air cleaner seen on this 1968 FLH was introduced in 1967. The motorcycle on the previous page is a 1966 model.

it an acceptable trade-off. Properly maintained and serviced, the Shovelhead was slightly better at keeping its oil supply inside the engine.

However, the Shovelhead would come to be widely maligned by some of the Harley faithful, for reasons often not connected to its design or engineering. The engine came to symbolize the acquisition of Harley-Davidson by American Machine and Foundry (AMF) in 1969. The Motor Company found itself in need of a substantial financial injection to produce more and better motorcycles for a growing market.

Unfortunately the "better" component suffered diminishing focus in the rush to regain a bigger piece of the pie.

Despite the money and management woes between Harley-Davidson and AMF, the Shovelhead would serve as the basic big twin for 18 years. The motor found application in every manner of tourer, cruiser, custom, chopper, police and racing configuration. And the Shovel generated an ever-widening aftermarket of speed and custom parts, so it remains the most-ridden example of pre-Evolution Harleys on the road.

In 1966 the Linkert
carburetor was replaced
by a Tillotson unit.

XLH Sportster **1966**

The overall configuration of the Sportster hadn't changed in seven years. In 1966, which would be the last chapter for kick-start only, the price of an XLH was $1,415. And although it was only $200 less than the Electra-Glide, the Sporty was in great demand as a smokin' street machine.

The XLH was still chunkier than the British challengers from Triumph, BSA and Norton. But with 60 horsepower and an adult portion of torque, the V-twin held its own, especially when the engine was tweaked for a bit more urge. The factory bump in the horsepower came

from new cams, pumper carburetor and better exhaust plumbing. The "ham can" air cleaner cover, fitted to meet federal emission regulations, was not generally considered an attractive addition.

MODEL XLH 1966

Engine Ohv 45° V-twin
Displacement 53.9ci (883cc)
Transmission Four-speed
Horsepower 45
Wheelbase 57in (1448mm)
Weight 505lb (229kg)
Top speed 105mph (169kph)
Price $1,415

245

1966 was the last year for the kickstarter on the XLH. The air cleaner is an aftermarket item.

In 1967 the XLH got a new battery/oil tank platform to accommodate the electric starter. As with the Electra-Glide, the battery pushed the oil tank to the right side, and everything was rubber mounted. Even with the addition of 30-some pounds (14+kg), the Sportster was still faster than it had been the previous year. The shock absorber spring adjusters were changed for a wider range of settings. The only significant styling change was the compact form of the new headlight nacelle, which included an indicator lamp panel for the oil pressure and ammeter lights.

Also, as proclaimed in the magazine ads, "The Neat-Pleat All-Model Buddy Seat has California styling that says 'class' from the word go!"

Most riders chose the rigid-mount seat and staggered shorty dual exhausts for the XLCH look. This 1966 XLH retains the traditional sport-touring configuration.

The Aermacchi Sprint
sired a family of scrambler
and flat-track race bikes.

CRTT Sprint **1966**

The generic road model of the Italian Sprint from Aermacchi spawned a family of scramblers, flat-trackers and roadracers in the US in the mid-Sixties. The competition-only scrambler was designated CRS. The 250cc four-stroke single was now straining its legs to keep pace with the two-strokes in roadracing. But on the dirt oval short tracks the Sprint could still carry the day.

In 1967 the Sprints received new aluminum barrels and heads, with shorter stroke and larger bore. The H model retained the large tank while the SS became the sportier street version with smaller fuel tank, rear fender and detachable headlight. The CRS remained the scrambler model and the roadracing rendition, with fairing, became the CRTT. For 1969 the stroke was increased to make the Sprint a 350cc engine, with the SS serving as the street version and the scrambler re-labeled the ERS.

The total number of Aermacchi Sprints imported from Italy in the period 1961 to 1974 is somewhere in the neighborhood of 40,000 machines, including racing models.

SPRINT PRODUCTION VERSION 1963

Engine Ohv single
Displacement 15ci (246cc)
Transmission Four-speed
Horsepower 26 @ 9000rpm
Wheelbase 52in (1321mm)
Weight 250lb (113kg)
Top speed 100mph (161kph)
Price $690

SS 350 **1969**

SS 350 1969

Engine Ohv single
Displacement 21.35ci (350cc)
Transmission Four-speed
Horsepower 25 @ 7000rpm
Wheelbase 53.3in (1354mm)
Weight 323lb (146.5kg)
Top speed 95mph (153kph)
Price $795

The Italian connection reached full-bloom in the late 1960s, when nearly half of Milwaukee's inventory was coming from Varese. The sportbike market was crowded with British, Japanese and European contenders, and the Harley-Davidson imports faced an increasingly sophisticated market that was discriminating about performance, technology and style.

Aermacchi's horizontal four-stroke single became a genuine giant-killer in Europe. In the hands of Kel Carruthers and Renzo Pasolini the rev-happy little singles humbled many of the traditional victors in continental roadracing. A small, powerful engine, hung low in a lightweight chassis, would outperform larger and more powerful machines on a demanding road circuit. In the meantime, the Japanese were applying this knowledge to two-stroke racers.

Milwaukee brought the enlarged 350 to U.S. riders as the SS 350 and CRS racing models. The street version weighed 323lb (146.5kg) gassed up and could top 95mph (153kph).

The 350 engine proved much
more powerful than the 250.

XR 750 **1970**

The XR 750 began as a de-stroked Sportster, replacing the KR 750 flathead racer. Even though Cal Rayborn displayed in convincing fashion the side valve's gumption at Daytona in 1968 and 1969, the need for more power had arrived.

Milwaukee was assailed in dirt-track racing by BSA, Triumph and Norton, who were joined by Honda, Yamaha and Kawasaki to make the roadracing more engaging. Under the direction of racing chief Dick O'Brien, the lighter and faster Sportster drew on the KRTT

and XLR for inspiration. The first XRs had iron cylinders and heads, with the exhaust pipes exiting low on the right. With the arrival of the alloy engine in 1972, the pipes curled around high on the left side and two carburetors poked out on the right.

The iron XR was about 100lb (45kg) lighter than a kick-start Sportster and made roughly 10 more horsepower in stock form. The ports, valves and cams got the racing treatment and the magneto went up front in place of a generator. Fuel was mixed by a Tillotson carburetor, and compression was only

XR 750 1970-80

Engine Ohv 45° V-twin
Displacement 45ci (750cc)
Transmission Four-speed
Horsepower 90
Wheelbase 57in (1448mm)
Weight 320lb (145kg)
Top speed 130mph (209kph)
Price $4,000

RIGHT: Tuned exhaust pipes exit high on the left side, out of harm's way when the machine is leaned well over and sliding at 100mph (161kph). This is not the original XR 750 which had the exhaust pipes exiting low on the right. Dirt-track tires provide the best balance between slip and grip.

8.5:1 in the interest of reliability. The motorcycle was fast but suffered serious overheating in long events, a deficiency most apparent in road races.

The alloy XR wasn't ready for Daytona in 1972, but its American roadracing career was effectively ended before it began. The impeccable Cal Rayborn took his old iron-head to England, without Milwaukee's blessing, and blistered the best of the British on tracks they knew and he didn't. The cool weather and short circuits matched perfectly the skills of Rayborn and the iron XR . He returned to the U.S. and

won the Grand National road-racing events at Indianapolis and Monterey on the alloy version. But thereafter, the two-strokes consigned the XR 750 to dirt-track racing exclusively.

There it has reigned, almost uninterrupted, ever since then. The XR 750 has become the all-time durability champion among production racing machines. Well, engines at least. The factory got out of the chassis business in the 1980s because racers were choosing their own frames, wheels and suspension components.

The aluminum cylinders and heads

contributed greatly to the new XR's ability to run stronger longer. The combustion chamber was improved and each was fed by a 36mm carburetor. Compression was up to 10.5:1. The rods, pistons and valves were all developed for the new engine, which had slightly less stroke and larger bore. Even though the cylinders were shorter than the iron ones, more and wider fins surrounded them.

The XR 750 continues its winning ways today, several times removed from the original Class C concept of production racing, but still a traditional 45° pushrod V-twin built to go fast.

FX Super Glide **1971**

When Harley-Davidson was acquired by AMF in 1969, several new models were already on the drafting table. One of them, penned by design director William G. Davidson, was the first attempt at a factory customized production roadster. And it was special enough to be christened with a name like Super Glide.

The FX 1200 Super Glide represented the response of Milwaukee, Willie G. in particular, to the spreading popularity of customs, cruisers and choppers on the motorcycle scene. Numbers of aftermarket performance and accessory makers had been established around the Shovelhead's platform, which didn't harm sales of the Electra-Glide. But Harley-Davidson reckoned there was a market for a moderately-styled production cruiser with a sporting flair. And it was right.

The Super Glide, as the FX designation suggests, was part Electra-Glide and part Sportster. The FL series had grown larger and heavier through the years, as the Sportster was becoming lighter and leaner. Somewhere in the

MODEL FX SUPER GLIDE 1971

Engine Ohv 45° V-twin
Displacement 73.73ci (1208cc)
Transmission Four-speed
Horsepower 65
Wheelbase 62in (1575mm)
Weight 560lb (254kg)
Top speed 110mph (177kph)
Price $2,500

The red, white and blue logo combined patriotism and Milwaukee's racing heritage.

middle, between porky and piglet, there was ground for a big-bore sport/cruiser. Some riders would revise and reshape the Super Glide to suit their own preferences, while others would be well served by the factory styling. Something for most everybody.

The FX combined the 74ci (1200cc) Shovelhead engine and frame with the Sportster front end. The electric starter was omitted, so a smaller battery was mounted on the right side. A European-style fiberglass seat/tail section was fitted, and a Sportster-type two-into-one exhaust system. The red, white and blue paint scheme reflected the current swell of patriotism in reaction to the Vietnam war. The new racing logo, a block numeral 1 in stars and stripes, decorated the top of the fuel tank. Ads touted the FX as the "All American Freedom Machine."

The concept was sound, although the boat-tail seat/fender was destined for early retirement. The prospect of European-style cafe racers achieving wide acceptance in the U.S. seemed at least a possibility in the early 1970s. But the Super Glide was hardly a backroads scratcher, and the tailpiece was over-sized to include space for a passenger. Set against the spare front end of the Sportster, the FX looked just like what it was – two different motorcycles. For 1972 the Super Glide had a standard rear fender, and sales began rising.

In 1973 the FX slimmed down even further when the wide 3.5-gallon (13.25lit) fuel tank was replaced with the slimmer tank from the Sprint. The suspension got stiffer springs and a disc brake appeared at each wheel, as the Super Glide became more performance-

Though the boat-tail styling was rejected, the cruiser concept won wide approval.

The instrument console holding the speedometer was mounted on the center of the gas tank.

oriented. Not that it was becoming a Sportster. In 1974 electric start was offered as an option (FXE).

The Super Glide is properly considered a seminal machine in the evolution of the Harley-Davidson Motor Company. It was the catalyst for a continuing variation of FX series machines, starting in 1977 with the Low Rider. Then followed the more retro Fat Bob and the custom Wide Glide, which begat the Sturgis, the Softail, the FXR sport model and the nostalgic Springer.

The FX series became more popular with each succeeding rendition, and provided a boost to Milwaukee's balance sheet as the Electra-Glide slipped against the wave of Japanese touring bikes. Most of the firm's styling and engineering emphasis focused on the FX models throughout the 1970s, and introduced the belt drive system that would later be adopted across the line.

RIGHT: The Super Glide wedded the Sportster front end to the rear end of the Electra-Glide.

Sportsters had
changed little
in ten years.
Aluminum
wheels
were optional.

XLH Sportster **1971**

The "ham can" air cleaner cover was not a popular addition to the Sportster. Staggered shorty duals replaced the stacked mufflers.

By 1968 the XLCH Sportster was outselling the XLH by two to one. High performance motorcycles were in demand as more new riders moved up from lightweight machines. The race was on for top honors in the power and speed categories, and new contenders from Japan challenged the current champs from the U.S. and Britain.

But while the XLH was in the process of looking more like the CH, and producing the same power, it was still outfitted in sport/touring trim. Windshield, saddlebags, and Buddy Seat were all available options, and one could still

MODEL XLH 1971

Engine Ohv 45° V-twin
Displacement 53.9ci (883cc)
Transmission Four-speed
Horsepower 50
Wheelbase 57in (1448mm)
Weight 505lb (229kg)
Top speed 105mph (169kph)
Price $1,980

RIGHT: Embroidered
patches have long been a
standard motorcycle
insignia. Harley-Davidson
logos featuring the bar
and shield emblem and
soaring eagles are
especially popular; all
proclaim brand loyalty.

choose the Low or High Ground Clearance style, which meant either 18- or 19-inch front wheel. The fork received an improved damping mechanism and increased travel. In 1968 the XLH sold for $1,650.

The heads were slightly redesigned for 1969 and got bigger valves, which with more efficient exhaust plumbing produced a five horsepower increase. In 1971 the Sportster was changed from a dry to wet clutch, which solved the problem of gear lube causing slippage.

The ignition points now moved inside the timing case, and featured an automatic advance mechanism. An optional boat-tail seat, a reduced version of the Super Glide tail, was offered in 1970 and 1971 but roundly rejected. Of course it's now a collector's item.

The Sportster's standard colors were black or birch white. The options were sparkling burgundy, turquoise, green, blue, red or copper. The buyer could also order the bike in gray primer and have it painted to taste.

In 1971 the Sportster was
fitted with a wet rather
than a dry clutch. A boat-
tail rear end was an
option, but it proved
unpopular.

RR250 **1972**

MODEL RR250 1972

Engine Vertical two-stroke twin

Displacement 15ci (246cc)

Transmission Five-speed

Horsepower 58 @ 12,000rpm

Wheelbase 55in (1397mm)

Weight 230lb (104kg)

Top speed 125mph (201kph)

Price Unknown

The RR250, a roadracing two-stroke twin from Aermacchi, appeared in 1971. Yamaha had demonstrated the speed and reliability of their two-strokes in world roadracing, but Walter Villa dominated the class from 1974-76. And in the third year he also collected the world 350cc championship.

The RR was built solely for roadracing, and neither Aermacchi nor Harley-Davidson offered a comparable road model. The early air-cooled engines made about 50 horsepower at 10,000rpm, but as development continued and water-cooling was added, the figure rose to 58 at 12,000. The otherwise identical 350cc version was said to produce nearly 70 horsepower.

Very few RR250 roadracers came to the U.S. Gary Scott rode one briefly for the factory, and Canadian Harley-Davidson distributor Trev Deeley fielded a team for several years. But the Aermacchi was soon outclassed by the rapid development in the world championship racing efforts of both Yamaha and Kawasaki. A few RR250s still appear in vintage races, but most are in museums.

This is one of
the RR250s fielded by
Canadian Trev Deeley.

XLH Sportster **1972**

Most Sportsters edged toward the leaner XLCH look in the 1970s. Seats varied from the straight two-place bench style to a curved "banana" seat to a stepped buddy seat. A new Bendix/Zenith carburetor improved the Sporty's starting habits.

The Sportster's development route had taken few turns in its first 15 years. The H and CH models became more similar than different, and the Superbike market was crowded with high-performance motorcycles from Italy, Britain and Japan. Time for more horsepower.

In 1972 the Sportster engine was bored to 3.18in (81mm) while the stroke remained at 3.81in (97mm). This brought displacement into the original Knucklehead realm, 61 cubic inches or 1000 cubic centimeters. In keeping with the European and Japanese

MODEL XLH 1972

Engine Ohv 45° V-twin
Displacement 61ci (1000cc)
Transmission Four-speed
Horsepower 50
Wheelbase 58.5in (1486mm)
Weight 530lb (240kg)
Top speed 116mph (187kph)
Price $2,120

RIGHT: Engine displacement was increased to 61 cubic inches (1000cc) in 1972 by enlarging the bore to 3.18in (81mm). The stroke remained at 3.81in (97mm).

emphasis on metric designations, the new Sporty was christened the XL 1000. The factory rating was 61 horsepower, meeting the popular standard of one pony per cubic inch. In the test by *Cycle World* magazine the new Sportster ran a 13.38 quarter-mile at just under 98mph (157.7kph).

The wet clutch got mixed reviews; engagement was good and only severe abuse would induce slippage, but lever effort was higher than before. An improved shifter drum in the transmission made gear changes more predictable, and the 530-pound (240kg) machine

was easy to ride. But the Sportster wasn't in the cozy corner anymore. The new look was naked aggression.

For 1973 both Sportsters were awarded a front disc brake. The new fork, from Showa of Japan, improved suspension compliance at the front, but better rear shocks remained several years distant. The federal government's safety program brought throttle return springs to the Sportster in 1974. Throttle controls had previously been simple push/pull cables. The horsepower rating remained at 61, but the XL 1000 was slightly quicker and faster than the 883.

The SX 350 fared poorly
against Japanese and
European dual-purpose
motorcycles.

Sprint SX 350 **1973**

The Sprint closed out its Milwaukee period with an on/off-road package called the SX 350. Although the four-stroke single had proven its merit in European roadracing and American dirt track, the civilian versions never captured the public fancy. As a trail bike it was outclassed by European and Japanese machines.

But it was cute, and different, and had a nice motor. Plus it was fast for a 350cc four-stroke single, and enjoyed a fair market among students, wanna-be racers and sport riders on a tight budget. All of which didn't add up to the numbers Milwaukee required to keep the Sprint in the lineup. Many of these bikes were ridden to rubble by less sensitive souls, or left to decompose behind the barn. But although parts are limited, some 50,000 Sprints were brought in from Italy during the 14-year run.

Collectibility is assured for the limited production racing models, but standard versions regularly appear on the market at reasonable prices. Sprints have begun appearing in some numbers at vintage races in the U.S., which may predict renewed interest in the road models.

SPRINT SX 350 1973

Engine Ohv single
Displacement 21ci (344cc)
Transmission Four-speed
Horsepower 25 @ 7000rpm
Wheelbase 56in (1425mm)
Weight 350lb (159kg)
Top speed 92mph (148kph)
Price $870

FLH Electra-Glide **1972**

The Electra-Glide was fitted with a front disc brake in 1972, adding needed stopping power to the heavyweight. The disc brought the FL a step closer to the mechanical mainstream, into which new and better technology was flowing faster each year. Even though the sales boom of the late 1960s had peaked, the market remained relatively strong and brand competition reflected equally dedicated competition. To the extent that the British were driven from the field.

Harley-Davidson was challenged not only to build better motorcycles, but a lot more of them as well. The AMF partnership was expected to accomplish that, and production did increase dramatically in three years. But the parent company decided that the Milwaukee facility lacked the capacity for greater output. So in 1974 the original factory was responsible for building engines and transmissions, while chassis construction and final assembly shifted to AMF's plant in York, Pennsylvania. This led to problems.

The transfer of final assembly to York was hardly a seamless matter. A three-month strike in 1974 put a serious crimp

MODEL FLH 1972

Engine Ohv 45° V-twin
Displacement 73.73ci (1208cc)
Transmission Four-speed
Horsepower 66
Wheelbase 61.5in (1562mm)
Weight 783lb (355kg)
Top speed 100mph (161kph)
Price $2,500

A die-cast metal
cigarette lighter in the
form of an early 1970s
Harley-Davidson FLH
touring bike.
Made in Japan.

in the production schedule, and other difficulties were at hand. Harley-Davidson was now confronted with a discontented work force, increasingly expensive modifications required by the government, the so-called Oil Crisis, conflicts between the old and new management, the arrival of the Honda Gold Wing, and quality control problems in the manufacturing and assembly processes.

Then, when it seemed things could hardly get worse, national motorcycle sales went into decline. But there was some good news.

Milwaukee management, abetted by increasingly hard-nosed road tests in the enthusiast press, convinced AMF that better motorcycles were required. And machines that looked a bit more contemporary. Approvals were issued, and the first of the next generation would arrive with the XLCR sport bike and FXS Low Rider in 1977.

Meanwhile the Electra-Glide was subjected to incremental modification. The horsepower rating for the FLH was 66 in 1973, and for 1974 Keihin carburetors replaced the Bendix units on the big twins.

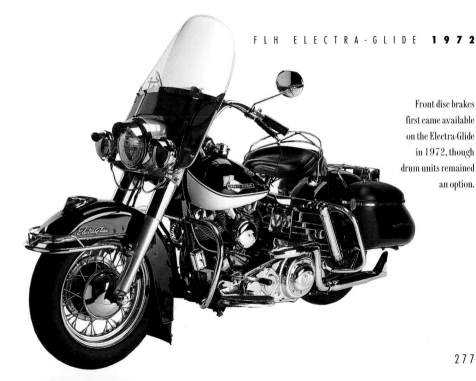

Front disc brakes
first came available
on the Electra-Glide
in 1972, though
drum units remained
an option.

SX & MX 250 **1975-76**

MODELS SX AND MX 250 1975-76

Engine Two-stroke single
Displacement 14.81ci (243cc)
Transmission Five-speed
Horsepower SX18, MX 32
Wheelbase SX 56in (1422mm), MX 57in (1448mm)
Weight SX 270lb (122.5kg), MX 233lb (106kg)
Top speed 90mph (145kph)
Price SX $1,142

The SX 250 was a large-bore version of the SX 175 introduced the year before. The Aermacchi two-strokes now represented Milwaukee's on/off-road offerings, since the four-stroke Sprints had been dropped from the roster. The 250 was created to combat the success of Yamaha's similar DT-1, but despite making reasonable horsepower, the handling and reliability were not widely praised. The two-strokes still had to battle against widespread dealer indifference, and the price/performance dominance of the Japanese machines.

In its final two years in the lineup, the

The SX 250 struggled to compete in the marketplace against purpose-built imports. The Aermacchi-built two-stroke SX 250 was discontinued in 1978.

Like the SX 250, the
MX 250 was outgunned
by Japanese machines.

250 was offered in a motocross version. Unfortunately the MX bike came in just as the sport had become an engineering study on long-travel suspension, and once again the dominant contenders were the Japanese manufacturers. Milwaukee did field a motocross team but the effort was short-lived.

In 1978 Harley-Davidson made the decision to concentrate on its traditional strengths and leave the lighweight market to others. The Aermacchi interest was sold to the Cagiva group in Italy, which built a broad-based motorcycle company that later included Ducati and Husqvarna.

The SX 250 had few components in common with the MX 250 motocross model.

XLCR Cafe Racer 1977

William G. Davidson had not been disheartened by the lukewarm reception accorded the styling of the first FX Super Glide when it appeared in 1971. He recognized that one design could hardly serve the requirements of two distinctly different sorts of motorcycle buyers. So, since the Super Glide was short on sportiness, he elected to base the next sport bike on the Sportster, and the next cruiser on the FX.

The former took form in the XLCR of 1977, a stark, Euro-style cafe racer (borrowing the British tag for a street racer) with a Sportster engine and modified chassis. The new frame took some design elements of the XR 750, with a box-section swingarm. Both upper and lower shock mounts were farther aft on the CR chassis, and allowed more room amidships for the battery and oil tank. Cast alloy wheels were fitted at both ends, with dual disc brakes in front and a single disc at the rear. The engine's black cylinders and sidecovers presented an imposing effect, and the siamesed exhaust system was, well...different. The design was said to produce an extra five horsepower.

MODEL XLCR CAFE RACER 1977

Engine Ohv 45° V-twin
Displacement 61ci (1000cc)
Transmission Four-speed
Horsepower 68
Wheelbase 58.5in (1486mm)
Weight 515lb (234kg)
Top speed 110mph (177kph)
Price $3,623

RIGHT: Black-on-black was
the motif for the XLCR Cafe
Racer. With its cast alloy
wheels and fiberglass
fenders and minimal
fairing, it looked the part.
And the quarter-mile
times were below 13
seconds.

The XLCR had the looks of a real sprinter for the twisties. The bikini fairing, low handlebars, racing-style seat, cast aluminum wheels and rear-set footpegs were all standard equipment for the civilian roadracers of the day. But in the 1970s, the real bad boys of the back roads had a sumptuous menu of street rods from which to choose. In addition to genuine cafe racers from Britain and Italy, the Japanese offered platforms with great heapings of horsepower in both four- and two-stroke engines. The XLCR was designed to appeal to this segment of the market, but once again

the effort was too little too late. The CR had little performance advantage to boast over a stock Sportster, and neither the chassis nor suspension were in line with prevailing sport bike performance standards.

Most dealers showed little interest in the XLCR, and some showrooms still contain the same machine that first rolled in 20 years ago. Now, of course, they are worth considerably more than they were then, despite the failure to generate much response among riders. The XLCR became a collector's item from the very beginning.

FXS Low Rider **1977**

Fortunately, the limited success of the XLCR was compensated for by the next member of the Super Glide family tree—the FXS Low Rider.

After a thorough survey of the custom/cruiser marketplace, Willie G. adopted the "less is more" credo of the times. The original FX had made the same gesture, but lacked the components for genuine sport-bike minimalism. The larger market for economy of design (and purpose) lived closer to the other side of the demographic chart, toward the chopper profile.

Thus the FXS. The junior Glide had produced steady 30 to 40 percent sales gains each year since 1973. The image of the backroads rambler had been supplanted by the outline of a boulevard brawler. The low-slung riding position, kicked back and looking cool, and the low seat offered chopper-style posture within easy reach of the tarmac.

By now the cruiser-bike styling had reached popularity levels that attracted other manufacturers. In a few years the

MODEL FXS LOW RIDER 1977

Engine Ohv 45° V-twin
Displacement 73.73ci (1208cc)
Transmission Four-speed
Horsepower 65
Wheelbase 63.5in (1613mm)
Weight 623lb (283kg)
Top speed 100mph (161kph)
Price $3,475

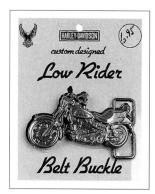

This official Harley-Davidson Low Rider belt buckle dates from 1980.

Japanese offered a series of semi-custom bikes but achieved little success. The notion of a machine with form as its primary function was sometimes difficult to grasp in cultures outside the United States.

The AMF/Harley-Davidson team had managed to double the production of motorcycles in four years. But the rush to put machines on the market had created difficulties in form and structure, in the motorcycles, the company, its dealers and their customers. Production and assembly quality control had been poorly observed, and unfortunately many machines were shipped in less than roadworthy condition. Which caused widespread moodiness.

Most of these difficulties had been solved by 1977, but the damage to reputation took some years to repair. The FXS, distilled as the Low Rider, accomplished for Milwaukee a tighter focus on the custom/cruiser style, and expanded the consumer base in substantial numbers. And the pattern was set for the next 20 years of variations on the theme.

Despite its parts-bin parenthood, the Low Rider emerged as the most coherently integrated motorcycle in the FX series to date. With its kicked-out Sportster front fork, deeply stepped dual seat and cast alloy wheels, the Low Rider looked both lean and muscular. It shared the front dual disc brakes with the XLCR, but had its own graceful two-into-one exhaust pipe, low-rise handlebars and the 3.5-gallon (13.25lit) fuel tank of the original FX. The lowered rear suspension brought seat height down to 27 inches (68.6cm). The Low Rider set the cruiser-look standard still in evidence today.

The traditional fat bob, dual fuel tanks were adorned with contemporary instruments, with the speedometer above the tachometer. Neutral indicator and oil pressure lights are up on the headlight nacelle.

FLH Electra-Glide **1977**

MODEL FLH ELECTRA-GLIDE 1977

Engine Ohv 45° V-twin
Displacement 73.73ci (1208cc)
Transmission Four-speed
Horsepower 66
Wheelbase 61.5in (1562mm)
Weight 750lb (340kg)
Top speed 100mph (161kph)
Price $3,865

Harley-Davidson celebrated its 75th anniversary in 1978. The occasion was marked by the arrival of the 80-cubic inch (1340cc) Electra-Glide, and anniversary editions of the the FL 1200 and the Sportster in black with gold striping. The Eighty featured the rocket-disc tank emblem of the late 1930s. Nostalgia returns.

Even though Milwaukee's overall sales had slipped nearly 30 percent, and the guys upstairs in suits were at odds over the company's future, work had proceeded on both new cruisers and tourers. The FLH 80 would head the effort to recoup some of the riders who had defected to Asian touring bikes. The baby Glides were expanding into more varied cruiser motifs, mixing styles of past and present. Despite the encroachment of economic recession, the game had grown more interesting.

With a slight increase in bore, and a larger one in stroke, the new Eighty recalled its flathead ancestor as big inch king. At a glance the engine was identical to the Seventy-four, but had one less fin on the cylinders and a huge ham-can air cleaner cover with 80 on the face. With cast alloy wheels,

The big twin got a new
dual-bucket saddle in
1977. The tank
nameplate is retro
(pre-AMF) as are the
tailpipes.

fairing, saddlebags and trunk the FLH-80 registered 750lb (340kg) on the scale. Although the big incher showed no power increase over the 1200, the stroker motor did produce more torque and

worked more comfortably with a large load. The sculptured, solid-mount seat was comfortable and not a long reach from the pavement. The FLH-80 went down the road in grand fashion, carried a passenger and fair amount of gear, and somehow combined the best of Milwaukee tradition, styling and unhurried performance. The new Eighty totaled 2,525 machines in its debut year, compared to 6,881 for the Seventy-four. Production rose to 3,429 the following year, but the engine also was used in the FX series and accounted for some 15,000 motorcycles between the Low Rider and the new Fat Bob model.

LEFT: The instruments were set in a console mounted on the gas tank. The speedometer is an aftermarket accessory.

FXEF Fat Bob **1979**

**MODEL FXEF FAT BOB
1977**

Engine Ohv 45° V-twin
Displacement 81.65ci
(1338cc)
Transmission Four-speed
Horsepower 65
Wheelbase 63.5in
(1613mm)
Weight 642lb (291kg)
Top speed 105mph
(169kph)
Price $4,260

The next model to slide into the custom/cruiser/chopper parade was the FXEF Fat Bob. The nickname came from the customizer's coinage for the first home-built cruisers with separate fuel tanks. Bobbed bikes with single tanks never got a distinctive moniker, other than choppers, and were never called Skinny Bobs.

The FXEF was a Low Rider with the choice of either 74- or 80-inch (1200 or 1340cc) engine, buckhorn handlebars, cast or spoked wheels, dual exhausts and a profile both long and lean. Once again Milwaukee had provided a

The Low Rider got a more muscular-looking brother with the FXEF Fat Bob. Foward-mounted highway pegs were mandatory for genuinely kicked-back cruising.

motorcycle cast roughly in the styling fashion adopted by its customers years earlier, offering a taste of specialized fashion to a wider audience. And in naming the factory fat bob the Fat Bob, adjoined by a symbol of trademark registration, Harley-Davidson staked legal claim to the name. The same was true for the labels Electra-Glide, Sportster, Super Glide and Harley-Davidson.

Concurrent with the arrival of retro-styling and factory folk art came the age of trademark protection. That story, which yet unfolds, has been, is and will be told elsewhere.

With Bob the FX series had grown to five models, which between them represented more than half of the Harley-Davidson production run (26,319 out of a total of 49,578). The Super Glide serial had come at just the proper time to write more chapters in the Milwaukee journal.

Internal corporate strife and an ailing economy had combined to revise the plans for Harley-Davidson's return to glory. As The Motor Company reached the end of its relationship with AMF, the sales figures remained reasonably stable. Total production for 1979 was just under 50,000, and dropped slightly in 1980. But in 1981, the year Harley Davidson returned to private ownership, the output would fall to under 42,000, and drop to only slightly over 30,000 a year later. The hard times had not yet ended.

LEFT: The Number One logo dates from the AMF era in Harley-Davidson's history. By 1979, this particular chapter was drawing to a close.
FAR LEFT: The FXEF had both speedometer and tachometer on the console. The 150mph limit on the speedo indicated Milwaukee's sense of humor.

FXB Sturgis **1980**

Hard times or not, Harley-Davidson had introduced new models each year during the AMF decade. Not entirely new from the ground up perhaps, but the company had demonstrated its commitment to remain a force in the motor- cycle market. And from the Milwaukee perspective, that meant machines which retained the traditional Harley appeal and also met higher standards of performance and reliability. So in 1980, classic style met contemporary technology in the form of belt drive. The newest rendition of the Super Glide was called the FXB Sturgis; B for belt and Sturgis for the South Dakota town hosting the annual summer gathering of the clans. The latest cruiser was another Wille G. creation in basic black with orange and chrome trim. The styling was immediately popular, but the rubber primary and final drive belts aroused suspicion. How durable would they be? What if they broke in the middle of nowhere? Valid questions.

But the return to belt drive proved out, because 70 years of development had

MODEL FXB STURGIS 1980

Engine Ohv 45° V-twin
Displacement 81.65ci (1338cc)
Transmission Four-speed
Horsepower 65
Wheelbase 64.7in (1643mm)
Weight 610lb (277kg)
Top speed 106mph (171kph)
Price $5,687

produced belts that could withstand considerable abuse. Manufactured by the Gates Rubber Company using Aramid nylon fiber, the belts provided quieter operation, required no adjustment or lubrication and outlasted steel chains. But replacement, when it was necessary, of the final drive belt was no simple matter, since it required removal of the primary drive and inner cover.

The new driveline also originated a new transmission with revised gear ratios. The new four-speed gearbox offered the tallest overall ratio (3.27:1) in the Milwaukee lineup, which meant 60-

mph (97kph) highway speeds at little more than 2500rpm. Acceleration was naturally less than brisk, but the Sturgis engine was relaxed in the element for which the bike was designed, easy cruising.

Once again Harley-Davidson had proceeded with caution in untested waters.

The Sturgis drive belt was developed by Gates Rubber Company, using nylon fiber for strength. The belts proved more durable than expected.

Only 1,470 examples of the Sturgis were made in its debut year, and production went to 3,543 the following year. The FXB accounted for only 1,833 bikes in 1982, its final year of production. But the Sturgis had met its design and performance requirements as a limited edition machine, and provided the test bed for the belt-drive system that would soon spread to other models.

FLT Tour Glide **1980**

Although the Sturgis drew attention with its brawny appearance and belt drive, the most important news of 1980 was the arrival of the FLT Tour Glide. Milwaukee had given its competitors something to strive for in the cruiser/custom format, and turned its attention to the the touring machine. But unlike the primarily cosmetic touches applied to the FX editions, the FLT was virtually a new motorcycle.

Only the Tour Glide's engine identified it with the FLH-80. With the next generation big twin still in the design stage, the interim fix was to bring the enlarged Shovelhead to a new standard of performance. Not in terms of more power, but by reducing chassis vibration and improving the handling. The engine featured transistorized ignition and a spin-on oil filter, and was buttoned to a new five-speed transmission.

The vibration and handling goals required a new frame and engine-mounting system. Harley engineers designed a three-point attachment system with rubber-shimmed mounts between frame and engine, which worked to absorb vibration. The swingarm bolted directly to the

MODEL FLT TOUR GLIDE 1980

Engine Ohv 45° V-twin
Displacement 81.65ci (1338cc)
Transmission Four-speed
Horsepower 65
Wheelbase 62.5in (1588mm)
Weight 781lb (354kg)
Top speed 95mph (153kph)
Price $6,961

RIGHT: The instruments were mounted on the forks. The fairing in front of them was fitted to the frame.
FAR RIGHT: The five-gallon (18.9lit) fuel tank was appreciated by FLT riders who planned long-distance touring.

transmission case, so the entire engine/drivetrain assembly was effectively isolated from the rest of the machine. The free-floating energy was directed to the rear wheel first by the new five-speed transmission. The more compact gearbox reduced the distance to the crankshaft, which allowed a shorter primary chain. And the final drive chain was fully enclosed and sealed. With full-time lubrication

it performed much longer without adjustment, and was also considerably cleaner. Supporting all this jiggery-pokery was a revised frame, distinguished by a protruding steering head and trailing fork. With the object of improving the heavyweight's low-speed handling, the engineers crafted an extended frameset with a steep, head-first steering stem set at 25 degrees. The set-back fork was canted at

28 degrees to offer enough trail for stability at highway speeds. The frame-mount stepped saddle fit lower in the chassis, putting the seat height at 29 inches (73.6cm).

The Tour Glide signaled that the design and engineering folks in Milwaukee had been busy. This was the first step toward building an entirely new motorcycle, engine included. The forecast for future Glides was in place; the 45-degree air-cooled V-twin would remain, in quieter and gentler form, in a contemporary chassis. All enclosed in traditional Harley-Davidson bodywork. Evolutionary.

The factory chopper had flame paint and the lowest seat in the lineup.

FXWG Wide-Glide **1980**

The Fat Bob got a broad brother in the FXWG Wide Glide, a Super Glide with the Electra-Glide front fork. The styling curve had swung from Electra-Glide to Super Glide to Sportster and back again. Whether by accident or intent, Milwaukee had created the perpetually circular design continuum. With three basic platforms alternating mechanical components and sheetmetal, the cross-pollination could continue indefinitely. As the identity of one model aged, it could adopt features of one or other sibling. A Möbius strip of infinite design variation.

Meanwhile, the appearance of the motorcycles notwithstanding, the task at hand was to make them work better. The Wide Glide also employed the 80-inch (1340cc) motor, which was now optional in the Low Rider and Super Glide. The Seventy-four engine was dropped from the lineup the following year and all the big twins were 1340cc engines. Once again the FX series accounted for more than fifty percent of the machines produced.

MODEL FXWG WIDE GLIDE 1980

Engine Ohv 45° V-twin
Displacement 81.65ci (1338cc)
Transmission Four-speed
Horsepower 65
Wheelbase 63.8in (1620mm)
Weight 586lb (266kg)
Top speed 102mph (165kph)
Price $5,683

FLH Electra-Glide **1981**

The 1981 FLH became the final Electra-Glide of the the AMF chapter in Harley-Davidson's biography. That may or may not confer upon it collectible status, but stranger things have happened. Much like the '65 Panhead, the final AMF/FLH represented an end and a beginning.

The signed copy in limited numbers for 1981 was titled the Heritage Edition, an appropriate term. The relationship with American Machine and Foundry had enabled Milwaukee to increase production and develop new models. But it had also created some scarred confidence among both dealers and customers, an issue the new owners were determined to address. A heritage restoration program.

New and better motorcycles were then half-way between the sketch pads and the assembly line. The new management team, thirteen former officials who had pooled their resources and borrowed lots of money, had to balance caution with daring. The sales of motorcycles had fallen in an economic recession, but new models were still arriving from Japan, meaning a smaller and tougher market.

MODEL FLH ELECTRA-GLIDE 1981

Engine Ohv 45° V-twin
Displacement 81.65ci (1338cc)
Transmission Four-speed
Horsepower 65
Wheelbase 61.5in (1562mm)
Weight 750lb (340kg)
Top speed 89mph (143kph)
Price $6,135

"The Eagle Soars Alone," a decanter celebrating the company's return to private ownership in 1981. Made in Germany.

The new Harley-Davidson Motor Company had to be a thoroughly modern example of efficient management, marketing, design, engineering and manufacturing. In order to meet those objectives, the new owners undertook a three-channel plan to control production costs and simultaneously ensure higher standards of quality control. Part of the new system gave factory workers more responsibility in the manufacturing processes. Against long odds, and after a four-year struggle, it worked. Harley-Davidson was back, same as it ever was but much better.

Sales of the Electra-Glide had averaged better than 10,000 annually for several years. But the flagging economy combined with efficient Japanese touring bikes cut the total to under 6,000 in 1982. Despite the improvements exhibited by the Tour Glide, the Shovelhead Electra-Glide suffered by comparison with the newest touring machines from abroad. The pace of evolution was forced to move more quickly. Entirely new versions of both FL and FX models had been approved for production, and were naturally the focus of attention in Milwaukee.

The 1981 Electra-Glide was the first non-AMF motorcycle off the assembly line. This is a limited edition Heritage model (784 built).

FXR Super Glide II **1982**

The first of the next generation middle-Glides was the FXR, which debuted in 1982 as the Super Glide II. The new chassis featured another version of the FLT frame, with a strong box-section backbone and rubber-mount system. The letter R distinguished the new model from the standard FX models, which retained solid-mount four-speed engines.

The five-speed 80-inch (1340cc) Shovelhead retained the lower compression first used in the FLT. The transmission was improved by revising the linkage and shift mechanism, which produced shorter lever throws and more positive gear changes and made neutral easier to select. Heim-jointed turnbuckles prevented the engine from rocking or twisting in the frame. The massive backbone and larger-diameter frame tubes provided a stiffer chassis.

The FXR was another product of established Milwaukee development paths. The engine had been upgraded first in the time-honored tradition of more displacement and more tractable power. Reliabilty was enhanced with improved lubrication delivery, better valve guides

MODEL FXR SUPER GLIDE II 1982

Engine Ohv 45° V-twin
Displacement 81.65ci (1338cc)
Transmission Five-speed
Horsepower 65
Wheelbase 64.7in (1643mm)
Weight 610lb (277kg)
Top speed 115mph (185kph)
Price $6,690

RIGHT: The 80in (1340cc) Shovelhead engine had nearly reached the end of its lifespan in the Super Glide II. But the new gearbox and mounting system was a welcomed advance from Milwaukee.

and electronic ignition. Then the new chassis came along to improve handling, comfort and overall performance.

The FXR matched the FLT for seat height (29 inches, 73.6cm), but its 31-degree steering head extended the wheebase to 64.7 inches (1643mm). A long motorcycle normally suffers some clumsiness at low speeds, and the Super Glide II was no exception. But at highway speeds it was impressively stable, and the new quotient of chassis rigidity allowed the FXR to handle twisty roads with considerable composure. Most testers agreed that this was the

best-handling big twin ever to come out of Milwaukee. Ground clearance didn't match the pure sport bikes, but within its limits the new model could straighten turns with new levels of speed and security. A cruiser that could scoot.

Fortunately the new handling standards were accompanied by better brakes. Two discs at the front and a dual-piston caliper disc at the rear elevated braking performance. Redesigned brake and clutch levers offered better leverage than previous controls. With form dialed in to Milwaukee's satisfaction, the function was coming up to speed.

This special edition
marked the 25th
anniversary of the
Sportster.

XLH Sportster **1982**

The Sportster was 25 years old in 1982. Naturally the occasion was honored with an anniversary edition, of which 932 were made in XLH trim and 778 in XLS configuration.

Sportster production was holding at about 8,000 per annum, but environmental regulations and low-octane fuel were not kind to high performance engines. For 1982 the Sportster's compression ratio was dropped to 8:1, with a consequent reduction in horsepower and speed. But it still weighed under 500lb (227kg) and could clip the quarter-mile under 14 seconds at 100mph (161kph), which was about the top speed. But the Honda CB900F was quicker and it cost about $1,000 less than a Sportster.

Even though elapsed times and speeds no longer figured strongly in the Sportster's marketing profile, price was another matter. The XLH retained its distinctive profile, featuring a lot of engine in a minimum of motorcycle, and still upheld its bad boy image after 25 years. But the job had grown more difficult, and the next year would see minimalism redefined in the XLX and a calculated drop in price.

MODEL XLH SPORTSTER 1982

Engine Ohv 45° V-twin
Displacement 61ci (1000cc)
Transmission Four-speed
Horsepower 50
Wheelbase 60in (1524mm)
Weight 515lb (234kg)
Top speed 100mph (161kph)
Price $4,670

The XR-1000 resulted
from requests for a
street version of the
XR-750 racer.

XR-1000 **1983**

No matter the national economic conditions, or the shifting fortunes of the motorcycle market, there always remained in Milwaukee a core group of hot rodders. In this instance it was marketing director Clyde Fessler, racing manager Dick O'Brien and design chief Willie G. Davidson. The result was the XR-1000.

Harley-Davidson had lost sizeable chunks of several market segments to the Japanese motorcycle manufacturers. Giving up the street rod market was rather like adding salt to the wounds. The high-performance fans had lobbied Milwaukee for years to build a street version of the racing XR-750, but to no avail. The XLCR had been considered little more than a cosmetic gesture. Real horsepower was the demand, in traditional Sportster trim.

The factory did consider the possibilities, but the costs involved in outfitting the racer for the street were much higher than projected sales would warrant. So the focus shifted to the existing Sportster, since the new chassis could handle more power and most of the necessary components were in house. Since the Evolution engine project

MODEL XR-1000 1983

Engine Ohv 45° V-twin
Displacement 61ci (1000cc)
Transmission Four-speed
Horsepower 71 @ 5600rpm
Wheelbase 60in (1524mm)
Weight 490lb (222kg)
Top speed 125mph (201kph)
Price $6,995

With 70 horsepower in street trim, the engine could be tuned for 95 on the track. As a road machine, it turned out to be troublesome,

had top priority at the time, the XR-1000 had to be a backroom project.

Dick O'Brien enlisted the aid of California flowmeister Jerry Branch, who made sure the new alloy heads breathed properly. Since the heads were larger, the new cast iron cylinders had to be shortened a half-inch (12.7mm) to fit the engine into the Sportster frame. The motor was rated at 70 horsepower, ten more than the standard powerplant. The XR-1000 was quicker (sub-13 second quarter-mile) and faster (125mph, 201kph) than the XLH, but was less than comfortable on the street. The potent engine made more mechanical clatter and stumbled at low speeds. And at nearly $7,000 the XR was costly.

Though no great success on the highway, the XR-1000 proved itself on the race track. O'Brien had the engine bolted into an old roadracing chassis, with competition suspension, brakes and full fairing, which was aptly dubbed "Lucifer's Hammer." Three-time national champ Jay Springsteen dusted the competition with it at Daytona. Later, under tuner Don Tilley and rider Gene Church, it went on to win three successive titles in the Battle of the Twins.

The real venue for the
XR-1000 was in Battle
of the Twins roadracing
competition.

The XLX-61 was a no-frills
motorcycle: not much
chrome, but a big engine.

XLX-61 Sportster **1983**

The XR-1000 did serve Milwaukee well as an image builder, and drew more than a few prospective customers into the show-rooms. Usually, after the oohs and ahhs had subsided, the viewers looked at the price tag and bought an XLX-61. By contrast, the baby brother from the bargain basement was an instant winner with the public. The XLX-61, with its traditional cubic-inch designation, was the Spartan warrior of the Sportster clan. And with a price below $4,000, it attracted much attention.

The XLX-61 Sportster recalled the "stripped stock" identification for early production bikes sold to amateur racers. The new Sportster was street-legal, of course, but for $3,995 it came with the bare minimum of accessories. Basic black was the standard color, with a solo seat, low handlebars

MODEL XLX-61 1983

Engine Ohv 45° V-twin
Displacement 61ci (1000cc)
Transmission Four-speed
Horsepower 56 @ 6000rpm
Wheelbase 60in (1524mm)
Weight 468lb (212kg)
Top speed 108mph (174kph)
Price $3,995

The XLX-61 was one of
Milwaukee's most astute
marketing maneuvers.
The price put the Sportster
within reach of more
riders, and brought more
customers into the
showrooms.

and little chrome. No instrument panel, tachometer, centerstand or sissy bar. Just a bare-bones machine with a big engine, a tribute to the concept of the original XLCH Sportster.

Harley-Davidson had got a bit too tricky with the XR-1000, but the muscle-flexing exercise earned points with the high-performance crowd and created another instant collectible. The XLX, on the other hand, grabbed the attention of riders who had given up on Milwaukee for simple economic reasons. When the price came down, they took another look and liked what they saw.

RIGHT: This commemorative eagle whiskey decanter was issued by Jim Beam in 1983, the year of the company's 80th anniversary.

CHAPTER 4

SURVIVAL OF THE FITTEST

FXST Softail **1984**

Evolution takes time. In the motorcycle business, money is also helpful. In the late 1960s, at the height of the motorcycle sales boom, Harley-Davidson had run out of time and money.

The Motor Company had survived Henry Ford, the Indian Motorcycle Company, the Great Depression, Hollywood and the Hell's Angels. But they were not prepared for Soichiro Honda. (Who knew?). American Machine and Foundry bought the time Milwaukee needed, and even helped finance the evolution. It took 15 years (a millisecond on the Darwinian scale), but by 1984 the newest member of the species had evolved.

Even veteran insiders had given Harley-Davidson little chance of success. A dinosaur, they concluded, that had reached the end of its natural lifespan. AMF, an apparent expert in the "recreation" business, had bailed out. The Japanese, who could design, tool-up and build entirely new motor-cycles in a period of 18 months, ruled the marketplace. Milwaukee was granted the proverbial snowball's chance in hell. Then hell froze over.

MODEL FXST 1984

Engine Ohv 45° V-twin
Displacement 81.65ci (1338cc)
Transmission Four-speed
Horsepower 55
Wheelbase 66.3in (1684mm)
Weight 628lb (285kg)
Top speed 110mph (177kph)
Price $7,999

RIGHT: The transition from the Shovelhead to the Evolution engine began in 1984. One of the five models with the new Evo motor was the FXST Softail. The rigid-looking frame section belied the shock absorbers cleverly hidden below the transmission.

To evolve is "to develop gradually by a process of growth and change." The Milwaukee process was nothing if not gradual. Threatened with extinction, Harley-Davidson was forced to adapt or expire. Once the decision was made, the experience could be put to work. The result of that effort was called appropriately, the Evolution engine.

Experience, that great teacher, showed that the new Harley-Davidson had to have a V-twin engine. And that the motorcycle must look, sound and feel much the same as Milwaukee iron always had. And further, that it perform to contemporary standards in terms of comfort, safety, maintenance and reliability. And maintain its resale value.

The story of how Harley-Davidson accomplished this feat has been recounted elsewhere. This book is merely a hardware history, the existence of which testifies that the New Harley-Davidson Motor Company achieved enormous success. The engine was the single most important part of Milwaukee's salvation equation. So how'd they do it?

Gradually, of course. They crafted an alloy engine with iron cylinder liners, squish band combustion chambers, flat-top pistons, stronger rods, closer tolerances, better oiling, tighter joints, stronger valve train, smaller valves set at 58 degrees, and computerized ignition. The result was a lighter, tighter, stronger, cooler, higher-power, longer-lasting and more fuel-efficient engine. The engineering was exhaustive, expensive and the testing was elaborate to the point of brutality. That done, the Evo team took two machines to Alabama's Talladega Speedway and ran them for four days straight at 85mph (137kph). They didn't break.

FLHTC

The V2 Evolution engine
proved to be the driving
force in the revitalization
of Harley-Davidson.

Electra-Glide Classic **1985**

When the Evo engine became the only big twin in 1985, design variations arrived to identify them by type and function. The FXRS Low Glide had the rubber-mount system, five-speeds, belt drive and triple disc brakes. The Heritage Softail joined the FL series in 1986, expanding the retro-look of the 1950s and retaining the solid-mount chassis.

Even though the Evolution engine received favorable coverage in the enthusiast press, the new models didn't claim overnight success. Not until 1988 did production approach the levels it had reached in the 1970s. Styling, market research and advertising employees took responsibilty for the next phase of the natural selection process.

The FLHT Electra-Glide Classic wore the traditional bar-mount fairing in 1985, and the styling was unchanged but for the old-time bar-and-shield tank emblem. An improved diaphragm clutch had been introduced the year before, designed for cooler running, less slippage and easier operation. With the five-speed transmission and belt drive, the big twins now required less effort of the rider.

MODEL FLHTC 1985

Engine Ohv 45° V-twin
Displacement 81.65ci (1338cc)
Transmission Five-speed
Horsepower 55
Wheelbase 62.9in (1598mm)
Weight 760lb (345kg)
Top speed 110mph (177kph)
Price $9,199

The Softail was joined by
a custom model in 1986.
Both had belt-drive.

FXSTC Softail **1986**

The FXST Softail, introduced in 1984, had struck the right balance of contemporary engineering and nostalgic design. Between the FX and FL renditions, the Softail accounted for nearly 9,000 machines in 1986. The rear frame section, designed to emulate the old rigid or "hard tail" frames, hid the shock absorbers beneath the transmission. And the new Harely not only resembled the old in appearance, with the engine solidly connected to the frame it rode more like its ancestor. Of course the Evo didn't shake with nearly the vigor of a Knucklehead.

The FX softie was presented in a custom version for 1986 (FXSTC), distinguished by the solid disc rear wheel, sissy bar, black engine and old-timey lettering on the fuel tank. The Custom accounted for 3,782 motorcycles, compared to 2,402 for the standard Softail. In 1987 the Custom outsold the ST better than two to one. Both the FX and FL Softails enjoyed early success and continued selling well in the 1990s.

MODEL FXSTC 1986

Engine Ohv 45° V-twin
Displacement 81.65ci (1338cc)
Transmission Four-speed
Horsepower 55
Wheelbase 66.3in (1684mm)
Weight 628b (285kg)
Top speed 110mph (177kph)
Price $8,460

Like the FXST, the Heritage
Softail hid its shock
absorbers out of sight.

FLST Heritage Softail **1986**

The Electra-Glide had added considerable bulk over the years, and the FX Softails had subtracted a few pounds in the cruiser category. Which meant there was room in between for an updated version of the Hydra-Glide. Enter the FLST Heritage Softail.

With the Evolution engine solidly in place (not rubber-mounted as it was in the FX series), the Heritage Softail mixed Milwaukee tradition with contemporary technology and design. The rigid-look rear frame section complemented the Hydra-Glide front end, with its deeply skirted fender, large headlight and sergeant-stripe cowling. The deeply stepped saddle reflected more modern tastes, and put the seat height at only 26.5 inches (67.3cm).

In the FLST Milwaukee had brought forth a modern classic, a retro-look with clean, uncluttered lines and modern, low-maintenance engine and running gear. The Heritage Softail was designed for stately motoring, which was reflected by the 1950s styling. Naturally it was followed a year later by the Heritage Softail Classic, with paint schemes from the past, rocket-fin mufflers, studded seats and saddlebags.

MODEL FLST 1986

Engine Ohv 45° V-twin
Displacement 81.65ci (1338cc)
Transmission Five-speed
Horsepower 55
Wheelbase 62.5in (1588mm)
Weight 650lb (295kg)
Top speed 112mph (180kph)
Price $9,099

This special edition of the
XLH 1100 celebrated the
Sportster's 30th
anniversary.

XLH 1100 Sportster **1987**

The Sportster was awarded an Evolution engine in 1986. The 883cc version was soon joined by an 1100 with larger valves and 63 horsepower, a ten-horse jump. The Sporties got new clutches and trannies, and a slightly revised frame.

In 1987 the XLH 883, including the lowered Hugger model, represented the bulk of Sportster production with 9,356 machines. The 1100 accounted for 4,618 bikes, 600 of which were the Anniversary edition shown here. The special celebrated the Sportster's 30th birthday with a black and chrome engine, orange and black paint and commemorative graphics.

The Hugger, so named for its abbreviated seat height, was aimed at women riders and males in the inseam-disadvantaged category. By shortening the fork tubes two inches (5cm), revising the shock absorber angle and offering a softer seat, the seat height came down to 26.75in (68cm). That was 1.75in (4.4cm) lower than the standard Sportster, and allowed more folks to plant their feet securely when stopped. A deluxe version of the 883 was also offered, with dual seat and wire wheels.

MODEL XLH 1100 1987

Engine Ohv 45° V-twin
Displacement 67.2ci (1100cc)
Transmission Four-speed
Horsepower 63
Wheelbase 60in (1524mm)
Weight 492lb (223kg) dry
Top speed 112mph (180kph)
Price $5,199

In 1988 the FXRS was
awarded a traditional fat
bob fuel tank.

FXRS Low Rider **1988**

With the Evolution engine powering the entire Harley-Davidson lineup, attention in Milwaukee turned to variations on the theme. A frenzy of new names and letters arrived to identify the assortment of Super Glide/Low Rider derivations that multiplied each year.

In 1985 the FXRS had returned with the longer suspension and dual-disc front brakes it had worn three years earlier. Now it was enhanced with the Evo engine and belt drive. The new version was slightly lighter despite the larger 4.5-gallon (17lit) fuel tank, and was rated at 55 horsepower. The price was $8,149.

By 1988 the Low Rider's popularity had been eclipsed by the Softail models, but performance-minded riders prefered the FXRS for its rubber-mount engine and sporting road manners. And they had the choice of more traditional styling in the standard model, which put the instruments on a tank panel rather than the handlebar. The Low Rider had a single disc brake on the front wheel and came standard with forward-mounted highway pegs. The turn signals were now attached to the mirror mounts.

MODEL FXRS 1988

Engine Ohv 45° V-twin
Displacement 81.65ci (1338cc)
Transmission Five-speed
Horsepower 55
Wheelbase 63.1in (1403mm)
Weight 580lb (263kg)
Top speed 110mph (177kph)
Price $9,245

The 1200 Sporster
produced more torque
and horsepower than
the 1100.

XLH 1200 Sportster **1988**

The Sportster climbed another rung on the muscle ladder in 1988 with the introduction of a 1200cc model. The 1100 cylinder bore was taken out to 3.50 inches (89mm), which combined with new combustion chambers, smaller valves and a 40mm carburetor produced 12 percent more power.

Naturally the 1200 was quicker and faster than its predecessor. The ratios between the first three gears had been tightened up the year before, which helped with acceleration. The new carburetor also featured an enrichening circuit that allowed smoother running in city riding and improved throttle response. The Sportsters also got the larger fork tubes awarded to the FX series, and for the first time came with two rear view mirrors.

For 1989 the Sporster roster remained at four models: the XLH 883 with solo seat and speedo only, with the price up to $3,999; the similarly equipped Hugger with buckhorn bars; the 883 Deluxe with wire wheels, dual seat and passenger pegs, and the 1200 with Deluxe accoutrements and more ponies. All models featured a new kickstand that was farther aft and an easier reach.

**MODEL XLH 1200
1988**

Engine Ohv 45° V-twin
Displacement 73.2ci (1200cc)
Transmission Four-speed
Horsepower 68 @ 4000rpm
Wheelbase 60in (1524mm)
Weight 490lb (222kg) dry
Top speed 112mph (180kph)
Price $5,875

The FXSTS Springer
successfully blended
vintage styling
with contemporary
engineering and materials.

FXSTS Softail Springer **1988**

Harley-Davidson took nostalgia another step into the past with the Softail Springer in 1988. Having made the rear suspension look just like the no-suspension frames of earlier years, Milwaukee decided to retro-style the front end as well. So the fork appeared to be right out of the 1940s, with the leading link/spring assembly characteristic of the Knucklehead era.

But while the look was 1948, the performance proved to be surprisingly contemporary. Harley engineers worked diligently to give the Springer fork modern manners on the road. And while they couldn't provide the same travel or damping provided by a telescopic fork, the result was a decent compromise between comfort and style.

With the help of computers, Teflon bearings and extensive testing, Milwaukee created a modern version of the design. Braking performance was acceptable, limited by the narrow front tire, not by the fork's design.

Once again Milwaukee tested the market with caution, building a total of 1,356 Springers for 1988. The styling was an immediate hit, and Milwaukee cranked up the production line for 1989.

MODEL FXSTS 1988

Engine Ohv 45° V-twin
Displacement 81.65ci (1338cc)
Transmission Five-speed
Horsepower 55
Wheelbase 64.5in (1638mm)
Weight 635lb (288kg)
Top speed 114mph (183kph)
Price $10,279

FLTC

Tour Glide Ultra Classic **1990**

Following the design and development efforts devoted to the FX series, Harley-Davidson refocused attention on the Electra-Glide. The FLHS Sport model was produced in limited numbers for 1987 and 1988, but didn't light large fires of enthusiasm with the sport-touring crowd. The FL Softail was far more popular.

For 1989 Milwaukee introduced the Tour Glide and Electra-Glide Ultra Classics, the Ultra indicating full-dress and then some. The Tour Glide featured the frame-mount fairing and the Electra-Glide retained the bar-mount fairing.

Both models got cruise control, 80-watt four-speaker stereo system with tuning controls for the passenger, CB radio/voice-activated intercom and fairing lowers.

The Ultras were distinguished by silver and black paint schemes, circular graphics on the tank and Ultra Classic nameplates on the front fender and saddlebags. All the touring models got new fuel tank designs, high-output alternator and self-canceling turn signals.

The luxury touring market, much like its automobile counterpart, had been

MODEL FLTC ULTRA CLASSIC 1990

Engine Ohv 45° V-twin
Displacement 81.65ci (1338cc)
Transmission Five-speed
Horsepower 55
Wheelbase 63.1in (1603mm)
Weight 780lb (354kg)
Top speed 110mph (177kph)
Price $13,695

RIGHT: The cockpit of the Tour Glide Ultra Classic was loaded with amenities, including CB radio, intercom, and an 80-watt stereo system. FAR RIGHT: Both rider and passenger were awarded comfortable seats. The rider's backrest is removable.

steadily redefined by the Japanese manufacturers. Electra-Glide sales were back on the rise and Milwaukee wanted to see that direction maintained. The popularity of long-distance touring, in considerable style and comfort, was showing signs of strength once again. Customer's requirements had expanded in hand with the manufacturers' abilities to produce deluxe machines. Amenities that Harley-Davidson had previously consigned to the aftermarket suppliers were now expected as original equipment. And passengers were now getting more attention than ever before. (If the saddlepal is unhappy, the rider is soon informed.) More creature comforts were being built into the pillion perch every year. Seat shapes and heights, backrests, armrests, footboards and grab rails all were reexamined and redesigned.

Touring, after all, is largely a family activity.

The Electra-Glide family came in for incremental revisions and improvements in 1990. The clutch was beefed, or maybe in this case porked, up and the cruise control was awarded some fine adjustment. The Electra-Glide, with its traditional bar-mounted fairing and small windscreen, had continued outselling the Tour Glide better than five to one. But in 1991, partly owing to Milwaukee's demonstration ride program at major rallies, the Tour Glide and its frame-mounted fairing picked up the pace.

Disc wheels and flared
fenders recall the
futurism of the '50s.

FLSTF Fat Boy **1990**

The evolutionary retro-revolution produced a chubby new member of the species in 1990, the Fat Boy. Genetically engineered with components from the Softail Custom and Heritage Softail Classic, the portly FLSTF was an instant crowd pleaser.

The Fat Boy took the Softail series into still another quasi-historical realm, the Flash Gordon era of science fiction space travel in the late 1940s. The silver custom dresser personified the ideal craft for solo inter-planetary travel, or a funky little shuttle for delivering recruits to distant outposts on the frontiers of the galaxy, or, in real life, to the diner across town.

Harley-Davidson had invented fantasy bikes from the factory, but the Fat Boy was still something of a first. The Super Glide, Low Rider, Fat Bob and Springer were all contemporary takes on historical or existing themes that were established, motorcycles modified to achieve a look. Derivative, in other words. The genius of the Fat Boy was not only that the look came before the machine, but that it emerged from a retouched Heritage Softail. New and old were combined not to replicate a motorcycle, but, by a

MODEL FLSTF FAT BOY 1990

Engine Ohv 45° V-twin
Displacement 81.65ci (1338cc)
Transmission Five-speed
Horsepower 55
Wheelbase 62.5in (1587mm)
Weight 665lb (302kg)
Top speed 114mph (183kph)
Price $10,995

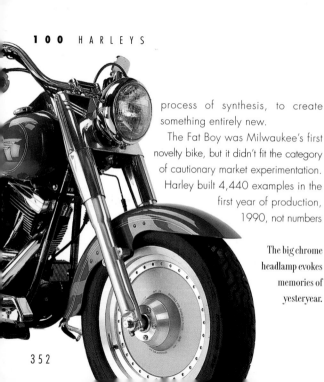

process of synthesis, to create something entirely new.

The Fat Boy was Milwaukee's first novelty bike, but it didn't fit the category of cautionary market experimentation. Harley built 4,440 examples in the first year of production, 1990, not numbers

The big chrome headlamp evokes memories of yesteryear.

associated with testing the waters. The Softail had already proven itself for four years running, so only the industrial-cosmic styling qualified as a risk factor.

Of course had it failed, the bike could readily be retrofitted with Heritage Softail components and probably not oversupply the market. But the production numbers indicate otherwise; that someone knew the brash Fat Boy would succeed on its own. That someone would be Willie G. Davidson, who designed this one for himself.

The Fat Boy underwent
few changes since its
introduction in 1990.
This 1996 model features
a new tank emblem.

Buell RR 1200 **1990**

**MODEL RR 1200
1990**

Engine Ohv 45° V-twin
Displacement 74ci
(1200cc)
Transmission Four-speed
Horsepower 75
Wheelbase 53.5in
(1359mm)
Weight 460lb (209kg)
Top speed 120mph
(193kph)
Price $13,695

This is a Harley from an entirely different hogpen. Actually only the engine is from Harley-Davidson; the rest originated in the imagination of ex-Milwaukee engineer Erik Buell. The handcrafted motorcycles are built in Mukwonago, Wisconsin.

Buell, a former roadracer, had been part of the design team on the FXR rubber-mount chassis. He had left Milwaukee in 1985 to build racing machines, one of which became a Sportster-engine Battle of the Twins

bike, appropriately called the RR-1000 Battle Twin. With the advent of the Evolution engine, the Buell in turn evolved as the RR 1200 in 1988, followed by the RS model with less bodywork. The Buell chassis is a birdcage frame of chrome-moly tubing, from which the Sportster engine is hung by a four-point mounting system. The mounts employ rubber dampers and Heim-joint rods to absorb the vibrations. A Marzocchi fork suspends the front end and a Works Performance shock

BELOW RIGHT: 1990 saw the 50th anniversary of the Sturgis, South Dakota motorcycle rally. The Buck Black Hills knife commemorates this event. The blade features a rally scene with a 22-carat gold overlay banner.

absorber, mounted below the engine, dampens the rear wheel. The exhaust pipe is also routed beneath the powerplant.

Most of the hardware is handmade for the sport bike, including the Buell-designed four-piston front brakes.

The wheel rims were furnished by Performance Machine, with spoke design and hubs by Erik Buell. The price of the RR 1200 was $13,695. Harley-Davidson later purchased part interest in Buell's company, effectively making it Milwaukee's sport bike division.

Echoes of the Vincent
Black Prince are evident
in Erik Buell's Harley-
powered RR 1200.

The Sturgis returned for
an encore in 1991 with an
entirely new chassis.

FXDB Sturgis **1991**

The Sturgis styling had been enormously popular ten years earlier, and now Milwaukee had the technology to present it in new and improved form. Thus the Dyna Glide chassis. The square-section frame backbone ran from the steering head to the swingarm pivot, and the engine-mount system used two rather than four rubber mounts. All major frame junctions were forged rather than stamped, and the oil tank was relocated below the transmission.

As a third-generation Low Rider, this version of the Sturgis was another limited edition model, built only a single year with a production run of 1,546. The reborn Sturgis served as a handsome platform to introduce the Dyna Glide chassis. The belt drive system had been simplified and improved since its inception, and now included an improved drive sprocket retainer that had better retention.

The new Sturgis resembled the original in most respects, but numerous differences appeared in the details. The Dyna version got only one disc brake in the front, and both the new seat and handlebar were higher than the old.

MODEL FXDB STURGIS 1991

Engine Ohv 45° V-twin
Displacement 81.65ci (1338cc)
Transmission Five-speed
Horsepower 72 @ 4000rpm
Wheelbase 62.5in (1587mm)
Weight 610lb (277kg)
Top speed 103mph (166kph)
Price $11,520

FXDB Dyna Daytona **1992**

The next model to carry the Dyna Glide chassis was still another limited edition, named the Daytona in honor of the 50th anniversary in 1991 of the Daytona 200. Released in 1992, the Daytona shared its running gear with the Sturgis but carried dual disc brakes in front.

The Daytona was heralded as the first Harley-Davidson to feature a true pearl paint. The two-tone scheme was gold pearl-glo with indigo blue metallic. The cast wheels and rear drive pulley were painted a complementary gold, and the tank featured a special 50th anniversary graphic. An inscription on the air cleaner cover also noted the exclusivity. The engine was finished in black and chrome.

The electrical components hid in a chrome-capped boxed under the seat's left side, where the oil tank formerly fit. The battery, also encased in chrome, sat in its original position on the right. The Daytona received Milwaukee's new self-canceling turn signals and a horn loud enough to wake up car drivers. The exhaust crossover pipe was nicely

MODEL FXDB DYNA DAYTONA 1992

Engine Ohv 45° V-twin
Displacement 81.65ci (1338cc)
Transmission Five-speed
Horsepower 72 @ 4000rpm
Wheelbase 65.5in (1664mm)
Weight 630lb (286kg)
Top speed 103mph (166kph)
Price $12,120

The Dyna Daytona was
a limited edition
commemorating 50 years
of motorcycle festivites at
Daytona Beach, Florida.
Production was confined
to 1,700 copies.

hidden away below the transmission. Other modifications included continuous venting for the fuel tanks to ensure constant fuel supply to the 40mm carburetor, which was recalibrated to make starting easier in cold weather.

The next version of the Dyna Glide would be designated the FXDC Custom. This model shared all the components of the Daytona, but was painted metallic silver and black, with a silver powder-coated frame. The Custom's engine was left unpainted. For 1993 the Dynas evolved as the FXDL Low Rider and FXDWG Wide Glide.

The FXRS was the most
popular model on the
Super Glide roster.

FXRS Low Rider **1991**

With the addition of the Convertible in 1989, the Super Glide/Low Rider family had grown to six models. The Low Rider remained the most popular member of the family, followed by the Custom and Super Glide. The Sport model, with its longer suspension travel, ran a distant third, but the Convertible was matching numbers with the standard FXR.

The Convertible was simply a Sport model with adjustable/detachable windshield and quick-release saddlebags. The dual-function option would later be used in similar fashion for the FLHR Road King. The Convertible was Milwaukee's rendition of a sport-touring machine, which was easily rigged to suit for either end of the functional scale. A motorcycle with fewer long-haul comforts than the Electra-Glide, and more amenities than the Sportster.

The motorcycle press held general consensus that the FXR Sport was the best handling and most versatile of all the big Harleys. Though a broad accord among the H-D faithful held that the motorcycle press was comprised largely of street-racing rabble and draft dodgers.

MODEL FXRS 1991

Engine Ohv 45° V-twin
Displacement 81.65ci (1338cc)
Transmission Five-speed
Horsepower 55
Wheelbase 63.1in (1403mm)
Weight 620lb (281kg)
Top speed 110mph (177kph)
Price $11,340

FXDWG Wide Glide **1993**

W ith the arrival of 1993 it was obviously time to celebrate Harley-Davidson's 90th anniversary in the motorcycle business. A large party was planned for Milwaukee, with group rides arriving from across the continent, parades, motorcycle races, rock 'n roll shows and assorted revelries. And six Anniversary Edition motorcycles.

Foremost among the commemorative models was the FXWDG Dyna Wide Glide. With its 32-degree fork rake, 21-inch front wheel and trademarked Ape Hanger handlebars, it was Fat Bob fashion revisited. Milwaukee had again

blurred the distinction between civilian and factory choppers. For more conservative cruisers, Harley-Davidson offered the FXDL Dyna Low Rider.

The Wide Glide represented a salute to the chopper revival of two decades prior, the kicked-out, laid-back Easy Rider posture of bike and rider. The minimalist's recliner for the open road, headed for adventure feet first. Maybe not the most comfortable posture for long hours in the saddle, but just right for cruising the back roads or boulevards. New motor mounts and support plates brought a reduction in vibration.

MODEL FXDWG 1993

Engine Ohv 45° V-twin
Displacement 81.65ci (1338cc)
Transmission Five-speed
Horsepower 72 @ 4000rpm
Wheelbase 66.1in (1679mm)
Weight 615lb (279kg)
Top speed 110mph (177kph)
Price $12,550

In 1993 Harley-Davidson's limited edition anniversary models were customized with special silver/charcoal paint, serialized nameplates and cloisonné tank emblems.

The bobtail rear fender housed a tucked in tail light ("Frenched" was the 1950s term). The slim front fender sat in the 8-inch (20.3cm) gap between the fork tubes, accounting for the Glide's wideness. From the custom "pillow-soft" seat to the forward-mounted shifter and brake levers was a long span for the short of leg.

The Anniversary Editions were all fitted with serialized nameplates, "jeweled" cloisonné fuel tank emblems and two-tone silver/charcoal satin-brite paint schemes. The FXDWG special was limited to 1,993 machines.

The fairing shielded
the instruments,
radio and rider from
the elements.

FLHTC Ultra Classic **1993**

Another of the six 90th Anniversary limited editions was the FLHTC Electra-Glide Ultra Classic, of which 1,340 were made. A new automotive-style cruise control, with a tap-feature for raising and lowering speeds was introduced, and a new American-made CB radio was installed. The silver/gray/black paint, cloisonné tank emblems and serialized nameplate put the Anniversary model price at $16,099. All the touring machines had the new oil pan below the engine, which afforded better oil cooling and a lower center of gravity. Maintenance was also simplified, and the oil was checked with a dipstick. The battery, formerly housed in the saddlebag, had a new position below the seat. The tourers also got the ergonomically contoured brake and clutch levers, for easier reach and better feel.

The saddlebag lids now permanently

MODEL FLHTC ULTRA 1993

Engine Ohv 45° V-twin
Displacement 81.65ci (1338cc)
Transmission Five-speed
Horsepower 72 @ 4000rpm
Wheelbase 62.9in (1598mm)
Weight 774lb (351kg)
Top speed 110mph (177kph)
Price $15,349

attached, received new hinges and a nylon tether. The guard rails surrounding the bags were redesigned for both strength and appearance. The new latch mechanism offered both secure sealing and ease of operation.

The Ultras (Electra and Tour Glide) shared with the rest of the FL series an air-suspension system at both front and rear. Air pressure settings at both ends could be balanced to accommodate varying loads and road conditons.

The Electra-Glide's jumbo travel trunk was hinged on the left, opening sideways.

The Classic was
some 25 pounds
(11 kg) lighter
than the Ultra.

The fishtail mufflers,
spoked wheels and
studded seat and
saddlebags echo an
earlier era.

FLSTC Heritage Softail **1994**

T he Heritage Softail Nostalgia was first shown to the public during Bike Week in Daytona Beach. It was quickly dubbed the Cow Glide for its natural cowhide inserts on the seat and saddlebags. The bovine motif was complemented by wide Dunlop whitewall tires on wire wheels and a black and white paint scheme. The Nostalgia was the only non-Anniversary model to wear the chrome and cloisonné tank emblems. The FLSTN shared the Fat Boy's "shotgun" dual exhausts. Also a limited edition, the production line rolled out 2,200 Nostalgias.

The Softails shared many of the engineering improvements to the controls and drivelines of the other models. The Heritage Softail Classic retained the vintage character of the 1950s with two-tone paint and studded seat and saddlebags. The Classic managed to look a bit like every big twin built since 1949, and what looked good then would look good again.

The Heritage Softail lacked the touring refinements of the Electra-Glide Ultra Classic, but it was lighter by 55 pounds (25kg), a tad faster and didn't cost as much. And it was easier to handle

MODEL FLSTC 1994

Engine Ohv 45° V-twin
Displacement 81.65ci (1338cc)
Transmission Five-speed
Horsepower 72 @ 4000rpm
Wheelbase 62.5in (1588mm)
Weight 719lb (326kg)
Top speed 110mph (177kph)
Price $13,340

This poster, by H&M Enterprises, celebrates Harley-Davidson's 90th anniversary in 1993, the year the Heritage Softail Nostalgia debuted at Daytona Beach.

around town. The stylish half-dresser marked its eighth year of production, and remained popular for several fundamental reasons. Between touring luxury and sport-touring compromise stretches the broad landscape of all-purpose big bikes.

The 4.2-gallon (15.9lit) fuel tank was sufficient for all-around travel, the seat was less than 28 inches (71cm) off the pavement and the motor felt good. The massive V-twin did not float in the middle of the chassis, but was bolted directly to the frame. For many more than a few Harley enthusiasts, feeling the motor

is a large portion of the appeal. The Heritage Softail delivered a balanced package of past and present, and put more than several Shovelheads in the classified columns.

The Classic arrived fitted with high-rise handlebars that sweep back to the rider and a king-size Lexan windshield. The Hydra-Glide fork cover and leather saddlebags were directly from the 1950s, and the fishtail mufflers dated back farther. The Classic was offered in black, red, blue, or two-tone victory red sun-glo, aqua sun-glo/silver, wineberry sun-glo or black/scarlet red.

The 1993 Heritage
Softail Nostalgia
was nicknamed the
Cow Glide.

VR 1000 **1994**

The 1994 VR 1000 was the first pure racing motorcycle Harley-Davidson ever built. Every other Harley racer, from 1915 through 1993, had been a modified production machine. The VR was purpose-built from the ground up.

Milwaukee has never been comfortable with the concept of pure-bred competition machines. Eighty years earlier the founders had been dragged mumbling into the racing game, convinced of its necessity only after Indian had captivated the sporting enthusiasts of the 1910s and 1920s.

But once installed in the Milwaukee hierarchy, the racing department proved itself a continuing resource of team spirit and public good will. People rode their motorcycles to the races, and supported their favorite riders and manufacturers.

Harley-Davidson had maintained its support of dirt tack, the traditional American fairgrounds racing, and built a few XR 1000 production-based roadracers. But nothing on Milwaukee's menu suited the demands of Superbike racing in the 1990s. At the upper outposts of "street bike" competition, the track-wise roadsters weigh 375 pounds

MODEL VR 1000
1994

Engine DOHC 60° V-twin
Displacement 61ci (1000cc)
Transmission Five-speed
Horsepower 135 @ 10,000rpm
Wheelbase 55.5in (1410mm)
Weight 390lb (177kg)
Top speed 170mph (274kph)
Price $49,490

RIGHT: The VR 1000 engine is a dual overhead cam, liquid-cooled, 60-degree V-twin with four valves per cylinder. Initial horsepower rating was 135 at 10,000rpm.

(170kg) and produce 150 horsepower. Handling and braking factors are tuned to millisecond response margins. All of which is enormously expensive to achieve.

With some money in the bank, Harley decided to build its second eight-valve racer, with an American engine, chassis and brakes. Engineer Steve Scheibe headed the team, and called in experienced help from NASCAR and Indy Car racing. The project took five years and produced a double-overhead-cam, 60-degree V-twin, with 4-valve heads, Weber-USA electronic fuel injection and liquid cooling. Power went by gear to a multi-disc dry clutch and through a five-speed transmission.

The first bikes used a Penske inverted fork and Wilwood six-piston brake calipers. The road model carried an Ohlins fork with titanium-coated stanchions. The body work was constructed of carbon fiber, and the factory listed the dry weight at 390lb (176.9kg). The production schedule was set for 50 copies of the VR 1000, the price of each listed at $49,490.

The VR first appeared on the racetrack for the Daytona Superbike race in 1994.

There were few illusions about the early chances, and teething problems were anticipated, but the motorcycle handled remarkably well. Top speed was not at the level of frontrunners, though rider Miguel Duhamel turned in good results on some of the tighter circuits. Results for the 1995 season were disappointing, and rider Doug Chandler had difficulty coming to terms with the machine. National dirt track champion Chris Carr was also on the team and showed a quick learning curve.

Rumors circulated during the off-season that management disputes in Milwaukee cast doubts on the future of the VR 1000. The factions split as they had a half-century before; the economic rationale perceives big-league factory racing as large expense versus small return. The sporting enthusiast segment says racing pays huge dividends in public relations, and puts the company logo on television. And wins hearts and minds.

New cylinder heads upped horsepower as the 1996 season began, but success on the track remained elusive. Chris Carr subsequently went back to dirt-track racing, and Harley hired Pascal Picotte as lead rider.

The Road King combined
modern engineering
with the styling of the
1965 Electra-Glide.

FLHR Road King **1995**

The F series has gone through more permutations over the years than any other Harley-Davidson. The Kings of the Road are in continuous process, with subtle changes in accessory groups, paint schemes and comfort amenities.

The FLHR replaced the Electra-Glide Sport in 1994. The new five-gallon (18.9lit) tank had an electronic speedometer and digital odometer mounted at the top. The passenger seat detached for kingly solo rides. Also detachable were the saddle bags and Lexan windshield, turning the highway monarch into a boulevard emperor.

The Road King also received the new big twin wiring harness featuring waterproof connectors; the accessory plug activated with an illuminated switch, and the petcock was vacuum-operated. Also in common with its big brethren was a taller overall gear ratio.

The Road King had an air-adjustable front fork and stout 11.5in (29.2cm) brake discs at the bottom of each leg. But despite the modern techno-trickery, with those wide whitewalls, from a distance you'd swear it was an Electra-Glide from the 1960s. It just works a whole lot better.

MODEL FLHR ROAD KING 1995

Engine Ohv 45° V-twin
Displacement 81.65ci (1338cc)
Transmission Five-speed
Torque: 77lb-ft @ 4000rpm
Wheelbase 62.7in (1592mm)
Weight 719lb (326kg)
Top speed 112mph (180kph)
Price $13,475

The FXDL Dyna Low Rider
set the seat even closer to
the road.

FXDL Dyna Low Rider **1995**

The Dyna Low Rider continued its role as the standard cruiser of the FX series. The machine appealed to both the creative customizers and the cruising comfort segments of a broad market. The easier riders now accounted for 35 percent of the street-legal motorcycles sold nationwide. And Harley-Davidson, which had effectively re-engineered the cruiser division, held the lion's share of the category. The imports were coming closer in terms of style, and even a greater portion of the substance than they had previously managed.

But, whether imitation is the highest form of either praise or incompetence, the derivatives lacked that intangible element of the Harley identity.

The Dyna Low Rider received an electronic speedometer in 1995, and seat height was down a half-inch to 26.5 inches (67.3cm). The 32-degree front fork maintained the long and low look, and the dual disc front brakes help decelerate the Dyna's 615-pound (279kg) mass. The FXDL was priced at $12,475 for solid colors, with a $75 premium for metallic paint and another $150 for the choice of two-tone paint.

MODEL FXDL 1995

Engine Ohv 45° V-twin
Displacement 81.65ci (1338cc)
Transmission Five-speed
Torque: 97nm @ 2350rpm
Wheelbase 65.5in (1664mm)
Weight 615lb (279kg)
Top speed 103mph (166kph)
Price $12,475

Buell S2 Thunderbolt **1995**

In 1993 Harley-Davidson became almost-half owner of the Buell Motorcycle Company. Milwaukee, in a refreshing bit of candor, admitted that its specialized factory sport bikes had achieved little success in the marketplace. Better to assist someone well-suited to the design, chassis and assembly requirements of those machines, with Harley-Davidson acting only as the engine supplier.

The timing was right. Buell was under-capitalized, Harley needed a sport bike and an investment opportunity. In 1994 the Thunderbolt was the first product of the new partnership between Milwaukee and Mukwonago. The chassis' wheelbase and steering geometry were unchanged, but the new design left more of both the engine and frame visible. The riding position became something of a compromise between the racer's crouch and the cruiser's slouch.

The Thunderbolt bristled with tasty techno-pieces, from the frame and engine mounts, huge disc brake with 6-piston caliper, inverted fork, to the subverted shock absorber and carbon-fiber air cleaner cover. The oversize muffler permitted some tweaking of the

**MODEL S2
THUNDERBOLT 1995**

Engine Ohv 45° V-twin
Displacement 73.4ci
(1203cc)
Transmission Five-speed
Horsepower: 76 @
5200rpm
Wheelbase 55in
(1397mm)
Weight 481lb (218kg)
Top speed 130mph
(209kph)
Price $11,995

The S2 adapts to sport-touring mode with the addition of saddlebags. The factory version, S2T, comes with fairing lowers and higher handlebars.

1200 Sportster's performance profile, and the horsepower rating bumped up to 76 at 5200rpm, with exactly matching figures for torque. The curb weight was 481 pounds (218kg). The production schedule was set for 300 Thunderbolts in its debut year.

In 1996 the S2T was introduced with color coordinated saddlebags and fairing lowers, with touring handlebars and footpegs. Another example of Harley-Davidson's support showed in the prices; the S2 listed for $11,995 and the touring model for $12,795, well in line with the competition.

The Buell S2
Thunderbolt features
a unique Uniplanar
rubber-mount engine
system and
underslung shock
absorber.

The 28-degree fork and long-travel suspension improved handling on the back roads.

FXDS Dyna Convertible **1996**

The FXRS Convertible Low Rider had proven more popular than its stablemate the Sport Edition. With the switch to the Dyna Glide chassis, the Sport was deleted in favor of the FXDS Convertible. The motorcycles had been too similar to warrant separate models, and without its windscreen and saddlebags the Convertible was a Sport.

The Dyna transition did effect some modifications to the sport-touring member of the Milwaukee roster. The steering head angle diminished from 31 to 28 degrees, and wheelbase shrank about an inch to 63.9 inches (1623mm),

giving the newer generation quicker handling in the tighter turns. And the Dyna had a quarter-inch (0.63cm) more ground clearance. But the FXDS also managed to gain 35 pounds (15.9kg) in the process.

The obvious appeal of the Dyna Glide Convertible, just as its predecessor, was the quick-change capability. The windshield and saddlebags detached readily in a few minutes, swapping the Convertible's character from tourer to boulevardier in short order. Most commuter and weekend riders, however, tended to leave the windshield in place.

MODEL FXDS 1996

Engine Ohv 45° V-twin
Displacement 81.65ci (1338cc)
Transmission Five-speed
Horsepower 72 @ 4000rpm
Wheelbase 63.9in (1623mm)
Weight 638lb (289kg)
Top speed 112mph (180kph)
Price $13,330

The FLSTN wears more
traditional garb than its
Fat Boy sibling.

FLSTN 1996

The Heritage Softail Special also carried over to 1996 relatively unrevised. Despite the new Fat Boy-style fired-enamel nameplate on the tank, the Special was some 70 pounds (31.7kg) lighter than the Softail Nostalgia of 1993. And the seat height, according to the factory specs, was two inches (5cm) lower. Like the Springer, the Heritage Softail built a loyal following among riders faithful to traditional Milwaukee style. With 16-inch spoked chrome wheels, whitewall tires and elegant two-tone paint scheme in traditional fashion, the Special recalled the pleasant days of yesteryear. Now made more pleasing by the presence of an easy-starting, oil-tight V-twin rumbling through its hardtail-style chassis.

The electronic speedometer may have seemed somewhat inconsistent with the retro-style of the FLSTN, but the laced leather seat and saddlebags and fishtail-tipped mufflers provided a balanced anachronism. The internal improvements for 1996 included a stronger and quieter transmission and weather-sealed connectors in the wiring system.

MODEL FLSTN 1996

Engine Ohv 45° V-twin
Displacement 81.65ci (1338cc)
Transmission Five-speed
Horsepower 72 @ 4000rpm
Wheelbase 63.9in (1623mm)
Weight 655lb (297kg)
Top speed 110mph (177kph)
Price $14,665

The Softail Custom runs
a kicked-out, 34-degree
front fork.

FXSTC Softail Custom **1996**

The Softail Custom also saw few revisions in five years but for color options and graphic trim. The spiritual cousin of the Springer was the kicked-out king of the crowd, with a fork raked at 34 degrees and 66.5 inches (1690mm) of wheelbase. The seat height was down to 26.6 inches (67.6cm). The Custom bore more resemblance to the original hardtail choppers of the 1950s. The laced 21-inch front wheel sat well out in front of the rest of the machine, and the buckhorn bars

and highway pegs invited the laid-back posture characteristic of the traditional feet-first style. The disc rear wheel was shared with the Fat Boy.

Unlike some of its siblings, the Softail Custom had become no more of a porker over the years, and in fact even lost a few pounds. Dry weight was 613lb (278kg). The Custom and the Wide Glide still employed 5.2-gallon (19.7lit) fuel tanks while the other FX models had the trim 4.9-gallon (18.5lit) units. For 1996 the Custom was offered in vivid black, patriot red pearl, states blue pearl, and three two-tone options.

MODEL FXSTC 1996

Engine Ohv 45° V-twin
Displacement 81.65ci (1338cc)
Transmission Five-speed
Horsepower 72 @ 4000rpm
Wheelbase 66.5in (1690mm)
Weight 613lb (278kg)
Top speed 110mph (177kph)
Price $13,630

With the XL 1200S,
the Sportster became
considerably sportier.

XL 1200S Sportster 1996

Since joining the Evolutionary family in 1986, the Sportster had been awarded doses of the technology advanced by the heavyweights. Belt drives and five-speed transmission were standard on both the 883 and 1200cc models, and in 1996 the Sporties had five models in the lineup.

The standard XLH 883 with solo seat, laced wheels and low handlebar was the price leader at $5,095, and the buckhorn-barred Hugger followed in line at $5,760. The two new members of the group were the 1200cc Sport and Custom. The latter featured a 21-inch wire wheel in front, 16-inch slotted disc wheel at the rear and an embroidered dual seat. The Custom got handlebar risers, chromed highlights and a fired-enamel tank emblem. This top shelf Sportster listed for $8,360.

The XL1200S offered to put more of the sport back in Sportster, thus its full moniker, XL 1200S Sportster 1200 Sport. All the 1200s shared common upgrades for '96; the more efficient high-contact transmission gears, better switchgear and 13-spoke cast wheels. Laced wheels became an option. The S model added several bonuses for the

MODEL XL 1200S 1996

Engine Ohv 45° V-twin
Displacement 73.2ci (1200cc)
Transmission Five-speed
Horsepower 63
Wheelbase 60.2in (1529mm)
Weight 512lb (232kg)
Top speed 120mph (193kph)
Price $7,910

RIGHT: The eagle with bar and shield combination has been crafted in nearly every sort of material, including neon tubing. This example adorns a wall in Tramontin Harley-Davidson in New Jersey.

corner-strafers on the back country roads. Adjustable suspension made its Sportster debut, with gas reservoir shocks and cartridge-type front fork from Showa. Both were adjustable for spring pre-load and compression and rebound damping.

To complement the newly compliant suspension, Milwaukee fitted the Sportster front wheel with two 11.5-inch (29.2cm) floating discs and

a redesigned master cylinder. The new braking system, in concert with Dunlop Sport Elite tires, gave new zeal and energy to the deceleration process. The slowing distance was compressed by better equipment and the feedback it offered the rider through the chassis.

The suspension, brakes and tires rendered the sporting Sportster a more stable and comfortable platform at brisk rates on the twisty roads.

The XL 1200C
Custom was another
new addition to the
1996 roster,

FLHTC UI Ultra Classic Electra-

**MODEL FLHTC UI
1996**

Engine Ohv 45° V-twin
Displacement 81.65ci
(1338cc)
Transmission Five-speed
Torque 77lb-ft @
4000rpm
Wheelbase 62.7in
(1593mm)
Weight 781lb (354kg)
Top speed 110mph
(177kph)
Price $17,500

Milwaukee unveiled its first fuel-injected tourer with the 30th Anniversary Ultra Classic Electra-Glide in 1995. The next year the Weber Marelli spritzer system was standard on the Ultra Classic Tour Glide and optional for the Classic and Ultra Classic Electras.

In addition to performance gains at all speeds, the injecta-Glides ran clean enough to meet the California emission standards without a catalytic converter.

Refinements include cruise control, an 80-watt stereo with weather band, and CB radio.

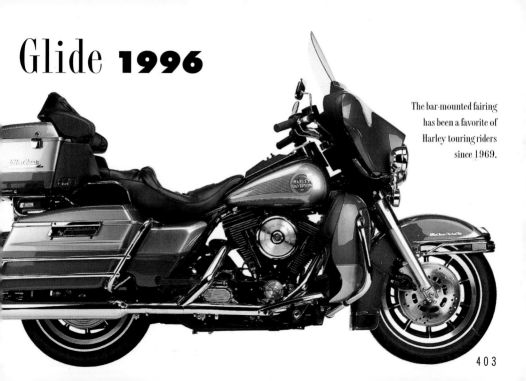

Glide **1996**

The bar-mounted fairing
has been a favorite of
Harley touring riders
since 1969.

RIGHT: The air cleaner proclaims this to be a fuel-injected version of the Ultra Classic Electra-Glide. Rider and passenger footboards are adjustable.

And fuel mileage went up by two miles per gallon (0.85km/lit) in city and country riding. The two-tone Tour Glide commanded a price of $18,160. With the optional injection, the Electra Ultra was priced the same, while the Classic Glide was tagged at $15,210 injected and $14,410 carbureted.

The Ultra Classic Electra-Glide naturally boasted features and amenities not found on the smaller, less expensive machines. Twin spotlights operated with the headlight's low beam, and running lights adorned the front fender and rear luggage. The AM/FM/cassette stereo

The Ultra Classic is
designed to accommodate
varying loads on the
open road. Front and rear
suspension are air
adjustable, with an anti-
dive system at the front.

had four speakers, a weather band and separate controls for the passenger. The built-in citizen's band radio featured a voice-activated intercom with helmet-mounted headsets. Electronic cruise control was also standard equipment.

The Electra-Glide has shown a steady curve of refinement during its years in service. The adoption of fuel injection heralds an even longer life for the venerable air-cooled V-twin. And given the Harley history of technological cross-pollination within the extended family of twins, fuel injection will likely appear on other models in the near future.

The Ultra Classic is advertised by Harley-Davidson as its top-of-the-line tourer. The instrumentation includes tap-up-tap-down electronic cruise control.

The Bad Boy is a leaner
and meaner cousin
to the Fat Boy.

FXSTSB Bad Boy **1996**

Introduced in 1995, the Softail Springer with-an-attitude traded chrome for the black outfit of the boulevard bandito. The Bad Boy wore the slotted disc rear wheel of the Custom and the smaller 4.2-gallon (15.9lit) fuel tank of the Springer. The studded, deeply-stepped saddle and forward-mount foot controls put the rider in the classic sit-up-and-beg posture. With seat height an inch (2.54cm) less than the Sportster Hugger, the rider sat more in than on the bike. The price was $13,850,

available in any color so long as it was black. Designer Willie G. Davidson has shown an affinity for black motorcycles, as evidenced by the XLCR and Sturgis.

The Bad Boy carried over to 1996 with only moderate revisions. More chrome had turned black, seat height dropped still lower to 25.75 inches (65.4cm) and the machine lost five pounds. The electronic speedometer arrived and the price went up by $575. The Black Bart color scheme remained the only option, but the tank and fender graphics were offered in choices of either yellow, purple or turquoise.

MODEL FXSTSB 1996

Engine Ohv 45° V-twin
Displacement 81.65ci (1338cc)
Transmission Five-speed
Torque 76lb-ft @ 3500rpm
Wheelbase 64.4in (1636mm)
Weight 635lb (288kg)
Top speed 110mph (177kph)
Price $14,425

Buell S1 Lightning **1996**

If anyone thought that Harley-Davidson's influence might cause Buell to go soft, the S1 Lightning answered their concerns. The sportier, and $2,000 less expensive, model got 10:1 compression, 91 horsepower at 5800 rpm and a curb weight of 440 pounds (200kg). That the Thunderbolt is designated S2 and the Lightning S1 indicates that sport performance had not been demoted as a priority.

Though the chassis are the same, the Lightning differs from the Thunderbolt in most other respects. The small windscreen, 4-gallon (15.1lit) tank,

seat/tail section and rear fender are unique to the Lightning, which is 25 pounds (11.3kg) lighter than the Thunderbolt. Add the 15-horsepower increase and the S1 takes a large stride in acceleration and speed. With the footpegs two inches (5cm) farther aft, the Thunderbolt rider adopts a posture closer to the racing crouch. The S1 turns in quarter-mile times under 12 seconds at 114mph (183kph), with a top speed of 130mph (209kph). With Harley-Davidson as partner, engine supplier and distribution network, the future of Buell's American sport bike looks bright.

MODEL S1 LIGHTNING 1996

Engine Ohv 45° V-twin
Displacement 73.4ci (1203cc)
Transmission Five-speed
Torque 91 @ 6000rpm
Wheelbase 55in (1397mm)
Weight 440lb (200kg)
Top speed 130mph (209kph)
Price $9,995

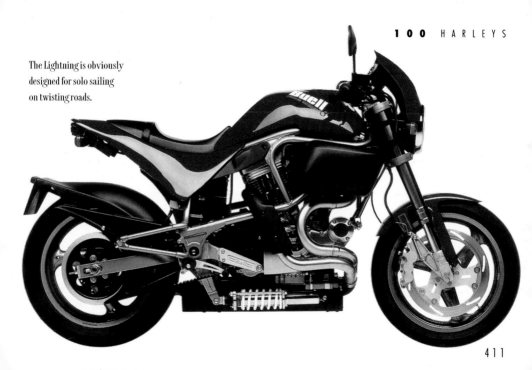

The Lightning is obviously
designed for solo sailing
on twisting roads.

PICTURE CREDITS

Unless otherwise identified in the following listing, the motorcycles pictured in this book were photographed by Neil Sutherland for Quadrillion Publishing. The publisher wishes to thank their respective owners for permission to photograph these vehicles. The credits are here given in page order.

CHAPTER 1

36-37: Illustration by Rod Ferring from a photograph courtesy of Harley-Davidson Archives, Milwaukee
38-43: Gene Calidonna, Seal Beach, California
44-49: Joy and Marv Baker, Vallejo, California
50-53: Dave Bettencourt, Gilroy, California
54-59: Jeff Gilbert, Los Angeles, California
60-61: Armando Magri, H-D of Sacramento, California
62-65: Bud Ekins, North Hollywood, California
66-67: Bud Ekins, North Hollywood, California
68-73: Mike Parti, North Hollywood, California
74-77: Daniel Statnekov, Tesuque, New Mexico
78-83: Harold Mathews, Mathews Harley-Davidson, Fresno, California
84-85: Armando Magri, H-D of Sacramento, California
86-89: Otis Chandler, Ojai, California
90-93: Armando Magri, H-D of Sacramento, California
94-97: Trev Deeley Museum, Vancouver, Canada
98-99: Trev Deeley Museum, Vancouver, Canada
100-103: Trev Deeley Museum, Vancouver, Canada
104-107: Otis Chandler, Ojai, California
108-111: Trev Deeley Museum, Vancouver, Canada
112-115: Armando Magri, H-D of Sacramento, California
116-119: Dave Royal, Nipomo, California
120-123: Mike Lady, Arroyo Grande, California

CHAPTER 2

126-131: Otis Chandler, Ojai, California
132-135: Dave Royal, Nipomo, California
136-139: Trev Deeley Museum, Vancouver, Canada
140-141: Armando Magri, H-D of Sacramento, California
142-143: Harold Mathews, Mathews Harley-Davidson, Fresno, California
144-147: Trev Deeley Museum, Vancouver, Canada
148-151: Armando Magri, H-D of Sacramento, California
152-153: Armando Magri, H-D of Sacramento, California
154-155: Trev Deeley Museum, Vancouver, Canada
156-159: Trev Deeley Museum, Vancouver, Canada
160-163: Fred Lange, Santa Maria, California
164-169: Oliver Shokouh, Harley-Davidson of Glendale, California
170-173: Trev Deeley Museum, Vancouver, Canada
174-177: Fred Lange, Santa Maria, California
178-181: Mike Lady, Arroyo Grande, California
182-185: Dave Royal, Nipomo, California
186-189: Trev Deeley Museum, Vancouver, Canada
190-192: Fred Lange, Santa Maria, California
193: John Tosta, Hanford, California
194-199: Fred Lange, Santa Maria, California
200-201: Paul Wheeler, Van Nuys, California
202-204: Harold Mathews, Mathews Harley-Davidson, Fresno, California
205-207: Otis Chandler, Ojai, California
208-211: Otis Chandler, Ojai, California
212-213: Doug Stein, Los Angeles, California
214: Bartels' Harley-Davidson, Marina Del Rey, California
215-216: Doug Stein, Los Angeles, California
217: Charles Holenda, Harley-Davidson of El Cajon, California
218-223: Otis Chandler, Ojai, California
224-225: Otis Chandler, Ojai, California
226-229: Sam Mathews, Mathews Harley-Davidson, Fresno, California
230-233: Randy Janson, El Cajon, California
234-237: Fred Lange, Santa Maria, California

CHAPTER 3

240-241: Paul Wheeler, Van Nuys, California
242-243: Mike Lady, Arroyo

100 H A R L E Y S